WITHDRAWN
FOR SALE

Ple...
date...
by ...

Wes...
Ser...

ww...

HOME WAS A GRAND HOTEL

HOME WAS A GRAND HOTEL

Tales of a Brighton Belle

Pamela Sydney Wilson

Book Guild Publishing
Sussex, England

First published in Great Britain in 2008 by
The Book Guild Ltd
Pavilion View
19 New Road
Brighton, BN1 1UF

Typesetting in Garamond by YHT Ltd, London

Printed in Great Britain by CPI Antony Rowe

A catalogue record for this book is available from The British Library.

ISBN 978 1 84624 259 5

Contents

Foreword   vii

Acknowledgements   ix

1   The Grand Hotel — Where it All Began   1

2   Pa — Early Days   7

3   Ma and My Early Years   13

4   Later Childhood Back in the Grand — Rules and Parties   21

5   Play and Pets   27

6   Christmas Time   37

7   Social Awakenings and Royalty   43

8   Brighton Beach, Heydays and Holidays   51

9   Strikes, Gangsters, Celebrities   57

10   Teenage Challenges and a Special Friendship   65

11   The Day War Was Declared   73

12   London and the Blitz   83

13   Best Part of the War — Lynton and Lynmouth, North Devon   91

14   Early WAAF Years of 2066191, Corporal Sydney Smith   99

15   11 Group Fighter Command and 'Y' Service   103

16   Buzz Bombs and Smog   113

17   100 Group Bomber Command, GIs and Glenn Miller   119

18   Colkirk, North Norfolk   135

19   Post-war Years — The Grand Re-opens   145

20   An Eye-opening Trip to Post-War Germany   163

21   New Beginnings   167

22   Grand Celebrations and Reunions   173

Afterwords   179

Dates   183

Foreword

A Tribute From the Author's Five Grandchildren

This book isn't just a story. These are the tales of someone special who has accomplished more than I could possibly imagine, through the highs of childhood mischief to the lows of being a young widow. Grandpam is the reason we, as grandchildren, can enjoy and share memories, and I am so proud to be part of them.

Susy, aged 25 years

I am so grateful to have been part of making this dream into a reality and help with recording some of the many stories about an extraordinary person's experiences. I can only hope that the readers of this book gain as much of an insight into my grandmother's life as I have been able to gain in my lifetime with her. We love you Big G.

Kim, aged 24 years

For my part, researching the archives at Brighton Museum was particularly illuminating. The big freezes of 1939 and 1947, the arrival of bananas for the first time since the start of the war, the stalwart Theatre Royal that remained open throughout World War II and the expansive *Evening Argus* spread on the 1984 bombing of the Grand

Hotel: just a taste of the social history that is the backdrop to this unique memoir.

Madeleine, aged 23 years

Still living in the city of Brighton and Hove where all the childhood adventures took place, it has been an insightful journey and pleasure to contribute to the publication of my grandmother's first book. It is an amazing record of her experiences of growing up inside a highly regarded hotel and living through the war which is becoming less and less imaginable to today's generation. Well done Grandpam!

Stephanie, aged 20 years

Congratulations to Grandpam for taking on the challenge of producing a historical book which is fascinating not only for us to read, but also for future generations of the family.

Alasdair, aged 18 years

Acknowledgements

When my father died comparatively young at 65, several friends commented that he should have written a book about his life in the hotel world. Sadly he never did so. This must be when the seed of doing something myself was sown.

Over the years I have scribbled memories and recollections on numerous pieces of scrap paper and old envelopes — whatever came to hand — but other events kept me from doing anything about putting it all together.

When I first came to Henfield, joining the local art club diverted my time, but in recent years I reluctantly had to give up driving and was no longer able to go 'painting out', which left a void. Eventually, with my son and daughter's persuasion and following my 80th birthday party at the Grand, which triggered so many memories, I started trying to put all the scribbled notes together.

Linda's help with sorting out the notes and putting them together chronologically as a book was invaluable. When I got started, her support, encouragement and our many delightful discussions made the 'writing' easier and gave us both great pleasure. I had begun by trying to type my story and then tried speaking it on to tape but neither method worked. However, once I began to put pen to paper it flowed and flowed!

That was the easy bit.

Linda then became my 'agent' and took over the majority of

dealings with our extremely helpful publishers and we have both appreciated the enthusiastic support of Antonio at the Grand Hotel. Robin became involved with good advice and guidance and my grandchildren were also all very encouraging — Kim, Stephanie and Madeleine helping with typing and research.

Support from brother Peter and niece Susan as well as my close friends Margie, Joan, Brian, Sheila and Christine, has also been very heartening — particularly as I found it unbelievable that they and family (and of course the Book Guild) had such faith that my 'witterings' would be publishable! Finally, the recent and unexpected bequest from my late cousin June has helped to make this project possible.

So thank you, thank you to all.

1

The Grand Hotel — Where it All Began

I was born Pamela Sydney Smith on the sixth floor of the Grand Hotel in Brighton in 1923.

The magnificent frontage of Brighton's Grand Hotel in the thirties. My father and I can just be seen standing by the entrance.

Today when I pass the Grand on Brighton seafront and the sun is shining on the gleaming white façade, I still have the same love/hate relationship for the old hotel that has been with me for most of my eighty-five years. It is like a gaudy wedding cake, laced with black wrought-iron railings on six levels of balconies, many of the windows staring blankly out to the English Channel. Perhaps the old lady looks her best at night when she is the largest jewel twinkling among all the lights along the seafront.

The hotel was built in 1864 and was the first hotel outside London to have lifts, known then as 'ascending omnibuses'. It was built on the site of the old West Battery which had several cannons pointing out to sea. Where the cannons once stood is the present small curved inner approach road — now a car parking area. Either side, Cannon Place and Artillery Street, which are now built over, bore witness to the military connection. The earliest West Battery fort was destroyed by a French attack more than a hundred years earlier.

The West Battery site, on which the Grand Hotel would be built. (Photograph courtesy of Chris Horlock)

The original fishing village of Brighthelmstone began to disappear around the middle of the eighteenth century and Brighton's popularity as a seaside resort increased with the patronage of the Prince Regent (who became King George IV in 1820), the building of his palace, the Royal Pavilion, the growing belief in the health-giving benefits of sea air and sea bathing, and the arrival of the railways in the mid-nineteenth century.

When my father began his career in the hotel industry in the early 1920s the Grand had become a very grand hotel indeed. The main entrance with an imposing rise of wide, white marble steps, flanked either side by gleaming brass handrails, brought you up to the revolving front door. There you were greeted by the uniformed commissionaire and various porters to carry in your luggage, and pages to do your errands. Inside the hall with its marble pillars and a deep-piled Turkish carpet were low round coffee tables, around which guests sat in armchairs watching the new arrivals with interest.

Towards the rear of the hall, on the left, the stairs begin to rise, forming an impressive stairwell. At the far end on your right as you go up is a wooden newel post topped by the carved oak handrail, gradually winding out to form the fine oak balustrade which continues right up to the sixth floor. With hundreds of wrought-iron

The Grand's entrance hall, with its elegant staircase — and the perfect banister for sliding down! (Photograph courtesy of *Sussex Life*)

uprights on each riser, the staircase has always been my favourite feature of the hotel. When my brother and I were young we were occasionally allowed to slide down on the silky oak banister rail from the first floor down to the hall.

The first disaster to befall the Grand in my lifetime was when the hotel was requisitioned by the military during the Second World War. The wanton damage caused by the Australian soldiers was atrocious and months of expensive refurbishment work was required before the hotel could be re-opened in late 1946.

The second disaster, when the Grand became famous worldwide, happened when, at 2.54 a.m. on the morning of 12 October 1984, the IRA bombed the hotel during the Conservative Party Conference, killing five people and severely injuring 34 others. The bomb had been placed in a bathroom on the fifth floor and blew out all the rooms above and below it. Margaret Thatcher, the Prime Minister, and her husband Denis had a very narrow escape but must have been badly shaken. The indomitable Mrs Thatcher carried on with the conference the next day — proving what a remarkable person she was.

Some readers may recall the television and newspaper pictures of the damage, when the hotel looked as if part of the centre had been sliced out — the top of where this space was had been my bedroom for almost all of my childhood.

At first I could only stare at the television pictures in total disbelief. Later that day I was hit by a mix of horror, shock and anger. Horror at the carnage and the dreadful suffering, shock at the mindless violence, and personal anger and indignation that 'my home' had been devastated. How dare the IRA blow up my bedroom!

It would add much to your understanding of my book if you could walk along Brighton seafront near the railings and look up at the Grand Hotel. You would be able to see where I sat as a child on the roof with the nightwatchman, spellbound by the lights on the two piers and all along the seafront from Hove to Black Rock. Should you gaze one floor down to my bedroom windows, the fourth and fifth in from the west side on the top floor, you would see exactly where the IRA managed to slice out four levels with their bomb in 1984.

In October 1984 an IRA bomb killed four people and destroyed much of the Grand Hotel. (Photograph Simon Dack/*The Brighton Argus*). My bedroom was above the black gaping hole blown out by the bomb placed in a bathroom two floors below.

Again a large amount of compensation was paid and the hotel was partially rebuilt, very much modernised and refurbished. Today it is one of the finest five-star hotels on the south coast.

2

Pa — Early Days

In 1920 my father, Sidney Thomas Smith, became Company Secretary to the Grand Hotel Company when he was only 24. The more I think about my father and his achievements in the hotel world, the less I seem to know about him and his origins. He had been born in Derby in 1896. His father was a carpenter and I have a strong memory that at some point I was told my grandfather mainly made coffins and that he was killed when he fell off his horse because he was so drunk! I never knew my paternal grandparents; Pa's mother died in childbirth — a common occurrence in those days. His father then married her sister Sallie and they had a daughter, Auntie Minnie. Minnie's husband, Harry Bale, who had been badly gassed in the First World War, worked for the Great North Eastern Railway Company — Derby town then being a large railway terminus.

Grandfather Smith died when Sidney and Minnie were young and money was in short supply. As children they had beer to drink instead of milk because it was cheaper. They lived in a small terraced house on a steep hill where I used to go and stay with my step-grandmother 'Old Sallie', Auntie Minnie and her husband Uncle Harry. Being in a small family house intrigued me — so very different to the Grand, it was quite difficult for a child to understand. I liked the feeling of security it gave me, and the home-cooked food was such a pleasure after the rather rich and somewhat monotonous menus which were our everyday fare.

In the kitchen there was a large black iron range, stretching across the whole side wall. A kitchen range consisted of an enclosed coal fire, supplying hot water to the stone kitchen sink, two ovens and a wide hob. Coal dust and smoke made it necessary to clean the whole unit frequently; called 'black leading', it was done by a little old lady known as Aunt Agatha who never seemed to move away from the warmth — sitting all day in a rocking chair doing 'tatting' (a kind of crochet) and never speaking. Every piece of bed and table linen owned by all members of the family was edged with tatting until quite recently — even I had a tablecloth decorated with it.

When I was an adult I was always aware that although Pa was kind to Sallie and Minnie, who occasionally came to stay with us in the hotel, he thought neither of them was very bright. In fairness, Sallie would have been quite an old lady by then. Minnie was always kind and friendly towards us as children, and my mother was fond of her.

I tell you all this because I wish I knew from whom and from where Pa had inherited all his intelligence and abilities. I have talked to brother Peter about this and to both of us the background is a mystery. We did know that, interestingly, three families — all Pa's cousins — came quite regularly to the hotel; they were the Macbeths and their son Colin (a little older than me), the Ringhams (who had a daughter about my age), and then there was a bachelor uncle who I remember had a very exciting sports car and took me for rides in it and for trips in the speedboat which was moored by the West Pier every summer. Certainly these cousins were all successful people — for example, Rex Ringham owned a coalmine in Chesterfield where they lived in a large house with several servants.

Father left school two years before the First World War aged 14 and became an errand boy, delivering for a wine merchant in Derby; later, he worked in the shop. This probably accounted for his interest and knowledge of wines which must have been an asset throughout his career in the hotel industry. During these years at home with his stepmother and stepsister he also earned money by going on a Saturday evening to Derby Station to meet the last train from London, which brought members of various repertory companies to do theatre tours in the Midlands. He would carry their luggage back to his stepmother's boarding house where they stayed — this was an important part of the family income. Pa's main form of relaxation — probably because no money was required — was to take long walks in the Derbyshire Dales. I went with him on a couple of occasions and he had obviously developed a strong affection for that beautiful part of the country.

The contrast between Father's surroundings and standard of living as a child and the life he was to lead later in the world of luxury hotels was extraordinary.

Towards the later part of the First World War he was conscripted into the army and became a lance bombardier when stationed in Dover Castle. At that time a close friend of his who was also a soldier, Marcel Courrouau, took him to meet his fiancée — my mother's sister, Dorothy May — and it was then that he first met my mother, Vera. When he was eventually 'de-mobbed' in 1919, Pa returned to his job with the wine merchants in Derby.

Whenever possible in the years after leaving school he continued studying, eventually taking the public examination to become a Fellow of the Chartered Institute of Secretaries (FCIS). This was about 1920, when he and my mother became engaged to be married. Shortly after proposing, he answered an advertisement in *The Times* for Company Secretary to the Grand Hotel Company in Brighton and was accepted — a remarkable achievement for a boy who had left school at 14. Indeed, he was very well-read and would say nobody was properly educated until they had read Adam Smith's *Wealth of Nations*! My parents were married in the September of 1920, quite soon after Pa had taken up his new post.

Working in the hotel industry, he rapidly developed into a brilliant organiser and leader. He had excellent communication skills, and was able to relate to guests from all social backgrounds, many with titles, and stars of stage and films. He became very popular with both guests and staff and also with his own board of company directors, never becoming either subservient or condescending.

Known as 'STS' in the industry, Father was very well-respected,

My father, Sidney Thomas Smith

but most staff were a little in awe of him; after all, their jobs depended entirely on his opinion of them and their work.

His social abilities were exceptional and must have increased with maturity. He knew almost every guest personally — many of course became regular visitors and a number of people, especially wealthy widows, made the hotel their permanent home.

He was also an extremely good sportsman. He was an excellent tennis player, and played a lot of tennis with the Frenchman Jean Borotra, known as the 'Bounding Basque', on the hard court at the rear of the Metropole Hotel next door. This was to give Borotra practice before Wimbledon, where he was in several finals and which he won in 1924 and 1926. Likewise, Pa was a very able golfer — no surprise, especially as he had spent so much time walking many miles across the Derbyshire Dales around Matlock.

The hotel had a large, well-equipped snooker room — where during the winter months he was always happy to be challenged to a game by any of the gentlemen guests. He also had dancing lessons, as did Peter and I, but it was not really his 'thing' — he was not particularly musical, which was sad as it was Mother's greatest joy.

When first married, my parents lived in a small flat in Lorna Road,

Hove, where they were very happy in spite of living so far away from their families. About a year or so later the worries started when rumours began about the possibility of the Grand Hotel Company becoming part of the hotel group, Spiers and Ponds — which it did. This was a large public company which owned about 20 hotels in the south and east of England. A historical note of interest is that in the winter of 1861, Messrs Spiers and Pond, who also had catering interests in Melbourne, sponsored the First All England Eleven cricketers to go on a tour of Australia — now of course the international exchange event, 'the Ashes'. Fortunately, Father's position as Company Secretary was secure and he was asked to live in the hotel. It must have been a great relief to them both — particularly as there was still a great deal of unemployment in the country following the end of the First World War and my mother was expecting my arrival.

3

Ma and My Early Years

My mother was born in 1893, eight years before Queen Victoria died. Thus, I believe, she was very much influenced by the middle-class Victorian values. At that time it was considered very important to have well-brought up children and to this day I can hear Mother saying, 'Children should be seen but not heard'. I felt she was sometimes a little remote and not very involved with my life. I remember being so thrilled on the rare occasions when she met me at school, as even at the age of five I was expected to catch the bus home on my own. I think she must have taken after her mother because my Grandpa Reynolds, who I knew well, was a very kind, loving and generous man.

The only memory I have of my maternal grandmother is of staying at my grandparents' home in Isleworth near Richmond one Christmas. I don't believe my brother had been born by then, so I would have been about three years old. I am sure Mother and I were on the first floor landing when Ma gave me a sweet saying, 'This is the last one, so you may have it'. My grandmother must have heard her say this and shouted out, 'Don't give it to the child, I want it'. What a very odd incident, and sadly all that I remember of my grandmother, except that she was a small, dumpy little lady and I was very nervous of her — as, I believe, were my mother and her two sisters. Dorothy May (Auntie Dor-Dor), who was the eldest by seven years was a happy and very attractive little lady. Vera, my mother, was the middle sister and Ellalina (Auntie Ellie), who was another three years younger, was clever, but somewhat rebellious. Ma was shy and timid but very musical. She went on to music college from school to become a fine pianist. For some years she taught children to play the piano and during the First World War she enjoyed playing to convalescent soldiers at a nearby hospital.

Following her marriage to Pa in 1920, the way my mother adapted to her life living in the Grand Hotel was quite remarkable. She was blessed with a very kind and sweet nature and I never heard her say a bad word about anyone. I know she was much loved by both guests and staff. The only occasions she became emotional were when she was worried about my father and, in spite of the constraints and her dislike of living in the hotel, my parents adored each other throughout their marriage.

My brother and I have wondered what she did with herself all day — she seldom took us out and was certainly unaware of the mischief we got up to when we wandered about the hotel as quite small children. Like many of her generation, she believed that being 'ladylike' was important — not in a snooty way or acting in anyway superior, but always being polite and pleasant to others, whoever they were. She was also upset and embarrassed by any vulgarity or coarseness. The word 'sex' was not in her vocabulary and risqué remarks or bawdy jokes were quite unacceptable. She was extremely prudish and even if a joke in a Christmas cracker was slightly vulgar she always smiled and said, 'I don't understand' — and no one ever *dared* to explain! As a result I left home to spend five years in the services as innocent about the facts of life as a new-born lamb — even at the ripe old age of eighteen!

I was pleased, however, to develop a much closer relationship with Ma after my father died. She was living alone in a flat near us in Brighton and she developed a wonderful friendship with both of her grandchildren, whom she adored.

I was born in January 1923 on the sixth floor of the Grand Hotel in one of the front bedrooms overlooking the sea — quite a momentous event, as I was the only baby to be born in the hotel since it had been

14

built in 1864. Father and all Mother's family must have been greatly relieved at my safe arrival, following a period of concern for my mother, who, having suffered twice from rheumatic fever as a child, had been advised not to have children. In those days it was considered a serious condition, likely to be followed by complications such as a weak heart. But my safe arrival and the subsequent joy became muted because I was a screamer!

In certain cases very little can be done about a baby who screams for no apparent reason, day and night. In my case, this lasted for one to two years, and for any mother it is a very difficult time, having endless sleepless nights and exhausting days. Today it is an accepted quasi-medical condition, known to exist on the female side of a family, caused by an over-active brain. In our family I am aware that we have had four generations of 'screamers' — Dorothy May (mother's elder sister), myself, my daughter Linda and her daughter Susy, and my son's daughter Stephanie. I have mentioned this in some detail because I believe in my case it may have sown the seeds of the mixed feelings towards me by my father.

Following my birth, my screams brought complaints from the hotel residents living in nearby rooms, to such an extent that my mother and father had to move away to rooms right at the back of the building — but even this was insufficient and eventually they moved right out of the hotel to a maisonette near Hove Station, where my brother was born some four years later. Fortunately he was not a 'screamer' but an easy baby — proving the point that it is related to females.

It was almost certainly difficult for my parents to cope with a young baby whilst living in the hotel. Although Pa would have been working fairly regular office hours as Company Secretary, Ma must have been alone during most of the day, and I don't think she had many friends living near. Taking a large pram in and out of the hotel would have been an upheaval with the lifts and steps. Even the well-meant interest of the lady residents with their constant enquiries about the new baby would eventually become intrusive. How she coped with the endless washing and drying of nappies, I can't

15

imagine — no doubt one of the chambermaids may have helped, but even so how and where were they dried?

Fortunately Ma always loved the sea and swimming. One of my earliest memories is being on Brighton beach, with my mother sitting in a deckchair at the edge of the water. We were to the east of the West Pier and in the front of the Grand Hotel. It was high tide, the pebbles formed a kind of shelf, and being a hot day, it was very crowded. According to Ma, I was paddling and must have stepped forward out of my depth when she saw only my sunhat floating on the sea — I had completely disappeared!

She said she got up from the deckchair and stepped into the sea but because she was in an advanced state of pregnancy she could not reach me. Several strangers came to our rescue and I have a vague recollection of a man bending me over to make me vomit up the swallowed sea water. Mostly I know I wanted my mother but couldn't get near to her as she was surrounded by strangers who had realised her condition and were rightly, of course, more concerned for her. I can still remember objecting furiously when a strange woman tried to dress me and insisted on fastening my liberty bodice (a kind of vest).

No doubt Mother, once over the shock, was able to explain where we lived and someone was sent to the hotel to fetch my father. He came hurrying down the beach to us looking very out of place among the many holiday makers with his dark office suit and tie. He would have been very concerned about my mother and probably blamed me for the incident.

Soon after this we moved out of the hotel to a maisonette in Denmark Villas near Hove Station, where Peter was born. I was nearly four years old and remember being very proud of my beautiful baby brother, who grew into an attractive blond blue-eyed child — the apple of my parents' eye. I recall the night of his birth probably because my very much-loved grandfather was there — he sat by my bed, trying to persuade me to go to sleep and explaining that my mother was too busy to come and say goodnight!

Grandpa Reynolds, mother's father, always held a special place in my heart and I loved him dearly. He used to come and stay with us frequently during my childhood and I believe that Ma was his favourite daughter. He was always kind and loving, ready to read stories to me, and would give me a silver coin on his visits, usually a half-crown (12½ pence today), saying, 'Slip this in your pocket and don't tell your mother.' I usually told her, being a very open and straightforward child, and she always insisted I gave it back again, saying, 'Grandpa cannot afford to give you money.' When I obediently did so, he always put it back into my pocket.

I was a bridesmaid at the wedding of my Aunt Ellie in Isleworth. Here I am on the left, with Grandpa Reynolds, my brother Peter and cousin June

I had dancing lessons in the hotel ballroom organised by a lady called Vera Garbutt, who held performances in the theatre at the end of the pier. On one occasion I was chosen to do a solo entitled the 'doll dance', wearing a red-and-white checked dress and a bonnet. It involved stiff but rhythmic movements to the music. Grandpa, who I believe was the only member of my family to come and watch me,

17

often reminded me how he could see me counting even from where he sat in the dress circle — it made him laugh but he said he was very proud of me all the same. The evening of the show was wet and windy but it didn't stop him walking all the way to the end of the pier to see his granddaughter's debut!

Above our maisonette in Denmark Villas lived an elderly lady called Mrs Rose, with whom my mother became particularly friendly. We — Ma, Peter and I —would visit her for tea and there were always little wobbly red jellies especially for me, which I liked.

I don't remember much about Mrs Rose except that she was made my godmother — rather odd because by that time I was four years old, a little too old to be christened, especially in those days when, because so many babies died young, they were usually christened as soon as possible. Strangely, I am pretty sure Peter was christened at St Andrew's Church in Hove — I wonder if I was 'done' at the same time? Anyway, I think Mrs Rose died soon after we moved away to Portland Avenue.

I believe Ma was very happy with our move to Portland Avenue because we had a garden and, even better, cows in the field at the end of the garden. In the mid-1920s much of the back of Hove was still fields. Peter and I relished the chance to play in our own garden — for the only time during our youth.

For me things were not so happy — I began at a horrible little school in Norman Road near Hove Lagoon run by two elderly women. My memories are of being sent to stand in the corner for what seemed like hours on end — always precariously balanced standing on a wobbly chair, facing bare walls and having my knuckles rapped with a heavy duty ruler. What I did wrong I don't know — except I did find doing 'pothooks' (lines and lines of letter shapes in my exercise book) day after day and hour after hour very boring. At some point I was left there to board when my parents went on holiday. I have no idea where Peter (then only two) went at that time.

The school dinners were equally unforgettable and unpleasant. The food was always undercooked — even the fish was full of blood

— and we never had any pudding or fruit but were given a piece of chocolate (supplied by the parents) with a slice of bread. Eight or so small children slept in a large bedroom and we were put to bed at six p.m. sharp. Outside the sun was still shining and to this day I can still hear the sound of the other children sobbing under the bed covers.

Mother took me to school, and on one occasion as we walked through Wish Park, I was fascinated by an old lady asleep on a park bench and wrapped entirely in newspapers. Ma explained that she had nowhere to sleep because she was too poor to have a home and the newspapers kept her warm. I don't think I was surprised by this but I was impressed by the newspaper. Many years later as a WAAF, freezing cold in a Nissen hut, I did the same thing and it was copied by all the other women in the hut. It worked beautifully, kept us really warm, and I became very popular overnight!

Quite often at the age of five or six, I was told to get on a bus and go to the Grand, where Ma would be with my father. I waited for the green bus on the seafront opposite the lagoon, where a small road sloped up from the docks to join the main seafront road, and at the time I was waiting there the workers would come up from the docks on their motorbikes. The junction was fairly dangerous and I suppose the men were careless in their hurry to get home and on two occasions I was an unwilling witness to a couple of serious accidents which affected me badly — so much so, that I refused to speak for a week or so after. I must have been in shock!

We left the house in Portland Avenue and moved into a flat briefly at the bottom end of Montpelier Road. When I was about six I started at Brighton and Hove High School (Girls' Public Day School Trust) in the junior school, which I liked. I made lots of girl friends there, a couple of whom I still see. I loved the garden and enjoyed the needlework and painting classes. I remember learning to read quite quickly, but I wasn't read to very much. In those days, there were no eye tests for children at school and I was eleven or twelve years old before anybody realised that I could not read many of our school textbooks — especially the Bible. Eventually I was seen by an eye specialist, who found I had very long sight and needed glasses for close work. By this time I was well behind my class mates and never caught up. My frustration caused me to be bored and naughty and fail exams. Fortunately I was quick and eventually became self-taught, always reading a great deal, but never mastering maths.

4

Later Childhood Back in the Grand —
Rules and Parties

During the years before returning to live in the hotel permanently, we visited often, always going in through the garage entrance at the back, into a wide corridor, approached by a flight of marble steps. These were flanked by black railings with well-polished brass handrails and not one, but two sets of double doors — presumably to keep out the smell of petrol and also to deter any unwanted individuals. Father's office was a large room with a big fireplace and a bed, which he slept in if events kept him in the hotel until the early hours of the morning. It was here that I was put to bed for a while to rest before getting dressed up to go to children's parties, especially around Christmas time.

Near to Pa's office was the ladies' cloakroom. The first room had dressing tables, mirrors and several armchairs and a cloakroom attendant dressed in black with a long white apron who was responsible for taking the coats of ladies who were visiting to attend a ball or banquet. Beside her on a small table was a large saucer into which the ladies would put her tips. Through a wide archway, there was a second room which contained several lavatories and a row of china handbasins, which were decorated with lovely flower paintings, fresh soaps and small hand towels which were changed for fresh ones after each use. I don't recall the attendant's name but she was a friendly person who loved to chat. I have a memory of returning to the hotel after being out with my mother and I was singing — well, sort of singing — a continuous monologue about three fairies who lived in a tree house that was built into the tree trunk, and they would wave to me from the different windows. I am sure I went into the loo singing, and was still singing even when I came out, and the lady in black was saying to my mother something about me being a child with a colourful imagination and that I should be allowed to continue singing! Mother was probably embarrassed — but I think I would have only been three or four years old.

On the day we arrived as a family, when the hotel was to become our permanent home, my most vivid memory is of the lift. It was a small, dark, oak-panelled room in the centre of the building smelling of polish and cigars, with a padded bench seat on one side and two thick ropes close together in the corner. This was the famous hydraulic lift — the first to be installed in a public building outside London. The proud operator was 'Old Tom the Liftman'. Smart in his uniform, he hauled on the appropriate rope causing the little room to rise upwards and go back downwards. The whole operation took place slowly as befitting such an 'elevating' event. It was fascinating, and Old Tom did his job with great dignity.

During those early years of living in the Grand up on the seventh floor, when Peter was about three years old and I was about seven, it was always being impressed on us by our parents that it was most important that we were on our very best behaviour at all times. In particular, we had it drummed into us that when we were in the lift and the dining room, 'children should be seen, but not heard'. We had to use the lift several times a day, but we were allowed to run down the stairs on occasions if the lift was full. It took 6 to 8 adults and we had to press ourselves against the panelled sides and keep well out of the way of the guests as they alighted at different floors, so getting up to the sixth floor seemed to take a long time. Mostly Mother was there with us, but if not, Old Tom kept a strict eye. The lift only went to the sixth floor, so we had to get out and walk up a flight of stairs to reach the seventh.

Following our first Christmas of living in the hotel I was given a special 8th birthday party and all my class mates from the High School were invited. It took place in the banqueting room and we sat at a long table, with me at the top end wearing my new primrose yellow party dress, surrounded by kind and attentive waiters. The table was filled with a magnificent array of crustless sandwiches, rich gâteaux, éclairs, meringues and a birthday cake. Balloons and crackers were everywhere and the tea was followed by a Punch and Judy show. I am sure all this made me very popular, if briefly, with my school friends. Many years later during the war when I helped at the children's parties at Colkirk in Norfolk, I remember seeing similar sumptuous spreads and I am ashamed to say my hunger pangs got the better of me, and I would help myself when I hoped no one was looking. I am sure some of the young waiters at my birthday party, all those years before, must have wondered at the unfair distribution of goodies in the world of 1931!

Reflecting on this particular party, I wonder to myself whether it wasn't more a public relations occasion for my father than a celebration of my birthday. Having not been at the High School for very long, I couldn't have known the thirty to forty girls who were invited very well — and they must have thought it was all very lavish.

Very occasionally, on our way home to the Grand, Ma would take me into Taylor's toy shop in Preston Street. It was a treasure trove of delight. Best of all was a large glass-fronted cabinet of dolls' house furniture, beautifully made and expensive — but as I never had a dolls' house and nowhere to put it, I don't remember being bought any!

Another favourite place near the hotel on my way home from school was the paper shop at the top end of the mews where Ma would sometimes buy me a comic. My favourites were *The Rainbow* and *Tiny Tim*, and in those far-off days they were printed in colour on good quality paper and had a lovely smell.

In the main dining room, the family's table was immediately on the right of the large doors next to the head waiter's desk. Most of our meals were eaten together as a family, but when I was older, breakfast was eaten by myself, unless Peter was home for the school holidays. The head waiter, Mr Raymond Pozzi, a tall, rotund and jolly Italian, had a high desk with the lid at chest level so there was no need for a chair. From this position, he could see guests entering the dining room, greet them and show them to their tables, and also of course keep a strict eye on the waiters across the large room.

I remember times when Pa would pick up a glass or a piece of cutlery, inspect it intently and, on finding a small smear, would polish it with his serviette or, to the embarrassment of Peter and me, hold it under the table and quietly attract Mr Pozzi's attention, who would then replace the offending item. In fact Pa had a very sympathetic relationship with most of the senior staff. On one occasion I remember he was particularly kind to Mr Pozzi who was upset after driving through the New Forest one night. He had hit a pony which had rolled across the bonnet of his car and subsequently had to be shot — the pony, not Mr Pozzi.

We lived in rooms on the seventh floor on the west side of the hotel. My bedroom faced the sea, with my brother's room on one side and Pa's dressing room on the other. My bedroom was very large and contained a huge mahogany wardrobe with a mirror on the front. On the other side of the room there was a washstand on which stood a large china bowl and jug with matching soap dish and toothbrush holder all covered with flowers. The chambermaid would take the jug away and fill it with it with warm water for me to wash in. I covered the inside of the wardrobe door with photos, cards and cuttings of all my favourite film stars from magazines and papers. There was of course no television then, only the radio, and my favourite programme was Arthur Askey's 'Band Wagon'. It is sad to think that when the hotel was requisitioned in the war and we had to leave so hurriedly, all the lovely things left behind were broken up by the soldiers billeted there.

Our sitting room also faced the sea and our parents' bedroom was at the back overlooking the town, next to a large and cold bathroom recently converted. We had coal fires because there was no central heating and the wind would whistle through our rooms. Our rooms were not self-contained, so there was no front door like a flat would have had. This was mainly, I suppose, because above us on the eighth floor there were dormitories where the chambermaids slept, which they reached by walking along 'our' part of the corridor to a staircase next to our WC (water closet). This bizarre arrangement must have been somewhat of an embarrassment to them and to my parents. In those days there were no en-suite rooms in hotels as there are today (apart from the luxurious suites of rooms often occupied by permanent guests, mentioned later). There would have been only 3 or 4 separate toilets to each floor and only 3 or 4 bathrooms — so it was quite usual to see guests in their dressing gowns walking along the corridors, carrying towels and toiletries!

Our WC was rather special. The large window had fine views of the sea, the West Pier and the promenade to Hove as well as a very impressive 'loo seat' of polished oak, rather like a low table with a large hole in the middle, with sides that stretched across from wall to wall. It was very cosy — nice and warm to sit on, and with plenty of space for books and magazines either side! The loo window was also a fire exit. Outside it, an iron ladder fire escape went down to first-floor level, with no safety rails whatsoever. Had it ever been necessary for any of the older guests to use it, I am sure some would have fallen to their deaths onto the flat roof at the bottom. This ladder was a great temptation to my adventurous brother Peter, who frequently climbed out of the window and went all the way down and then back up again. To my knowledge this very dangerous exploit was never discovered by my parents, who, it seems, lived in total ignorance of our childish adventures throughout the hotel.

All the toilets in the hotel were the same and the only other place I have seen a seat like these was years later in Arundel Castle — which I also have good reason to remember. My friend Margie Pett (née Miller) and our respective husbands went to a ball at Arundel, and at one point in the evening, Margie and I wandered off through the castle to find a loo. After what seemed a long time we eventually found one and as it was pretty large and spacious we spruced ourselves up and sat next to each other to have smoke, but when it came to leaving we couldn't open the door. We rattled the handle and banged on it with no success, so we had another cigarette and waited to be rescued — thinking that our dear husbands would notice we were missing and come searching. No such luck. But after more banging and shouting, an unknown female heard us and was able to open the door from the outside. Very relieved in several ways, we thanked her profusely and returned to the ballroom. Much to our disgust no one had even missed us — Frank (my husband) and Basil (Pett) were still happily drinking with their friends, showed no concern and treated the whole episode with great hilarity.

The first and second floors, where the most expensive rooms in the hotel were, had unusual features known as communicating doors. These were 2 sets of doors with a small space between — thus, several rooms could be accessed without going out to the public corridor. You could have 2 or more bedrooms adjoining with a bathroom and toilet between them and an even larger room from which beds and wardrobes were removed and replaced with settees and armchairs, turning them into sitting rooms — this was always with all rooms facing the sea and with larger balconies. Several suites were permanent homes for wealthy guests.

Above us in the centre of the roof was a row of small rooms known as the 'Pigeon Holes', where the page boys slept. During the summer, quite late in the evening, I would go up and sit on the roof with the nightwatchman to gaze down at the lights on the two piers and all along the seafront. I would sit with my nightie wrapped round my knees, while he would have a cigarette with his brass hat next to him on the roof. One of his duties was to make regular patrols of every floor of the whole hotel, clocking in hourly on each floor to record the time.

5

Play and Pets

Living so high up we became accustomed to the south-westerly gales blowing all round us and the wind got under the wide corridor carpet, causing it to rise and balloon up several inches in the middle. I invented an unusual game when this happened. The carpet became a rough sea and the brown lino either side was land. I was the princess who had been shipwrecked and Peter the hero who had to rescue me from the wild sea and drag me safely on to the land. Eventually the game was forbidden when Peter banged his head on the large oak chest, causing a huge lump to appear on his forehead. The doctor was called and I was blamed and sent to my bedroom, very upset because I adored my little brother.

Spitting over the stairwell was another of our favourite games — and we both became rather good at it. I don't think we ever shared this fun with our friends, no doubt well aware we had to be careful never to be found out. We would stand, leaning slightly over the banister on the sixth floor, and with the biggest gobs of spit we could manage we spat down the stairwell — aiming for people's heads as they walked through the hall below. In particular we targeted father's very large, shiny bald head. If we succeeded we never knew because it was necessary to step out of sight just in case we hit the target and Pa looked up to see what was happening. A further refinement was to aim at the cups and saucers on the tea trays carried on upturned hands by the waiters. Our ingenuity for inventing unusual games seems to have been endless.

With less finesse, my brother got into real trouble for letting his football go over the banisters and down the stairwell, having been playing with the page boys on the seventh floor. I don't remember anyone being hit, but Father found out and was very cross. One of the page boys, Danny Hughes, as a schoolboy had been lightweight boxing champion of Sussex for two or three years and my father arranged for him to teach Peter how to box. Peter has always maintained that this helped him at boarding school and in the Navy. He became an ordinary seaman living on the lower deck with other young men, most of whom had not had much education, and Peter would help them write letters home to their families and girlfriends. Probably because he was both a charming and good-looking young man, the other chaps christened him 'Grace'.

Another of Peter's less harmless activities was to spread sand from the red sand-filled fire buckets over the ballroom floor. He did this with the aid of various school friends who had been invited to tea. It was probably after the second or third time this happened that Peter was duly sent to boarding school. Not surprising when you think how hard it must have been to remove all that sand from the highly polished ballroom floor before a dance due to take place the same evening.

My activities concerning the ballroom were certainly less disruptive. I would take friends down to show them what it was like in the space beneath the ballroom floor. First I showed them the old blue-and-white-tiled walls which were part of Hobden's Royal Baths, which had replaced the original Artillery Baths built in the early nineteenth century. Apparently the new 'modern bathing establishment' was officially opened in 1865 by the Mayor of Brighton and the guests were entertained in the Grand Hotel which had been opened eight months earlier. I showed my friends how the ballroom floor was supported by brick pillars set on the floor of the pool itself. Sadly, both the pool and a large function room known as the Hobden Room were lost when the hotel was re-built after the IRA bombing in

1984, but I understand the new leisure centre in the basement was named the Hobden Health Spa.

I then endeavoured to explain how the sprung dance floor operated. Fitted below the wooden floorboards, under the huge dance floor, was a complicated system of springs, so that when people were dancing the floor moved up and down with the music and movement.

Most times when I went down there in the early evening all was quiet, but years later if I was there during a dance the effect was extraordinary — very noisy, with the springs rising and falling as a hundred people or more danced above. If we were on the balcony above the ballroom watching a very crowded dance floor you got the impression of a sea of heads waving in time to the music. I know when I was older and actually dancing there, it did occur to me that I and my dance partner might suddenly slip down and disappear into the depths below!

Living so high up on the seventh floor never worried us as children, though I do recall there were safety bars across the sitting-room windows. But our bedrooms had very deep dormer windows which meant there was at least three feet of wall either side of the deep sill. This made us feel safe from the storms and strong winds blowing in from the sea. When the really bad south-westerlies blew and a lot of rain came in, George Watson, my father's personal valet, came and put sausage-like sandbags across to prevent the water soaking the carpets below.

George's other duties involved going to Pa's dressing room and laying out the clothes he would change into every evening — Pa had to look immaculate at all times. He would wear formal evening dress — a dinner jacket and black tie — most evenings, except when there was a large function such as a banquet or a ball, when George would put out his black tailcoat and pin-striped trousers. At weekends, Mother always wore a long evening dress when she went down to have dinner with my father. Usually she had a very pretty, pale grey chinchilla fur cape round her shoulders as the hotel lounge was often draughty. She looked so pretty with her bright blue eyes.

29

Ma and Pa at a formal ball in the Grand Hotel's ballroom

It would have been soon after the seventh floor became our permanent home that I became very fearful of being alone after dark. This occurred when Mother left us to go down to have dinner with Pa. I don't think Peter was affected in this way, although he was much younger than I was. I would be in bed with the door ajar to let in some light from the corridor, but that was no help. After a while I would ring the bell for the chambermaid to come, and tearfully beg her to fetch my mother, who came up from the dining room, leaving my father to finish his meal alone. She would try to settle me down. When this didn't work I would have a drink of water from a glass always left beside my bed and (I now believe intentionally) spill it over the bed, then I would ring for the maid again who sent over yet another message for Ma to come up to me. But this time it was often Father who came and was very angry with me.

I suppose to the adults I did seem just a very naughty child, but you can imagine how far away my parents were and how alone I must have felt in the silence of the seventh floor. In an ordinary

30

house a child would have been able to hear their mother and father moving about (and perhaps a radio on) immediately below them — whereas the seventh floor was a very long way above the ground floor in the hotel.

I think that Ma was very aware that the circumstances in which we lived were in many ways utterly unsuitable for bringing up children. She often told me how much she wanted to live in a country cottage with a large garden and have animals — dogs and cats and even chickens. I think this must have been why the cows in a field at the end of our garden in Portland Avenue excited her so much. We did have a dog when we lived there, but only briefly because it was run over by a car and killed as we were walking along the pavement in Church Road, with Peter in his pram.

Apparently whilst poor Ma was trying to deal with this horrid incident, Peter (who would have been about two) ate a whole bag of bananas, including some of the skins and the paper bag! I do remember a man kindly removing the corpse of the dog and putting it in a field, because the next day several girls at school kept asking me if the dead dog they had seen was mine. Maybe I recall it all so clearly because not long before I had witnessed those 2 terrible motorcycle accidents near the Lagoon in Hove.

When we lived in the hotel Mother did try to introduce a bit of 'natural normality' into our lives; a goldfish in a bowl swimming around in endless circles was one of her ideas. Unfortunately this was not very successful, as for some unknown reason the fish always seemed to die and when Pa asked her what she had done with the dead fish she confessed to putting them down the lavatory! This made Pa rather cross, and the resident plumber was called, who eventually reassured him that it was very unlikely the dead fish might appear in the lavatory basins on the floors below used by the hotel guests! Some years later my brother confessed to over-feeding the poor fish. But the reason for the deaths of a succession of canary birds was never discovered. After that we all had to wait several years before any more animal life became part of the family.

When we were old enough to be trusted to walk sensibly along the seafront, dogs were introduced. Before the war at different times we had 2 or 3 Scottie dogs all called 'Jock'. Most of the exercising, however, was undertaken by page boys — some of whom quite liked doing it on a fine day, but others, when it was raining or even snowing, did not do it so willingly. Strange as it may seem, I do not remember being either surprised or upset by the sudden disappearance of our pathetic menagerie!

During the school holidays Ma was very insistent we both had our daily dose of fresh air and exercise, whatever the weather. Well wrapped up, we were on our honour to walk as far as the 'angel' and back. This is the peace statue on the seafront marking the boundary between Brighton and Hove. Much of the time we found this very tedious, so I invented a game in which we listed to each other all the things we would do or buy if we had £100 — a huge amount of money (then aged ten years old, my pocket money was 6d. a week) — so that was great fun and made time pass quickly. In today's terms that was probably a kind of retail therapy!

During the August bank holiday weekends before the Second World War, crowds would gather along the seafront to see the pearly kings and queens. They came in large numbers from London and strolled along with many of their friends and families, their costumes sparkling in the sunshine. These were the cockney costermongers from London's East End. In order to be one, you had to be a cockney born 'within the sound of Bow Bells' — as recalled by the old nursery rhyme which refers to the fifteen bells of London:

'Oranges and lemons,' say the bells of St Clement's,
'You owe me five farthings,' say the bells of St Martin's,
'When will you pay me?' say the bells of Old Bailey,
'When I grow rich,' say the bells of Shoreditch,
'When will that be?' say the bells of Stepney,
'I do not know,' say the great bells of Bow ...

The holiday was a great day out by the sea for the cockneys and each district was represented by their own pearly kings and queens, who proudly wore clothes covered with pearl buttons sewn on every spare inch of every piece of clothing, including the men's caps. They collected coins for various charities and were sometimes given pearl buttons by the locals, which were much appreciated.

Frequently, both fairly drunk and disorderly, they became very much part of the bank holiday excitement and atmosphere. Sadly this custom came to an abrupt end due to the complete destruction of the East End during the first weeks of the London Blitz. It was Hitler's main objective, as he believed the bombs would persuade the cockneys to demand that the government make peace. He could not have been more wrong.

My old school friend Margie Miller recently recalled another exciting occasion when a very famous black American jazz pianist stayed in the Grand. Margie had come to tea, and after tea we were having our usual wander around the hotel to see if anything inter-esting was happening. We were nosing about near the ballroom entrance when we heard this fantastic piano music and as we edged ourselves just inside the ballroom doors to see and hear more, a loud American voice called, 'Come on in girls, let's meet you.' We could not have been very old and were wearing our green school tunics, cream shirts and school ties — not exactly visions of glamour — but the huge black man could not have been kinder. With him were two more large black men and we were a little nervous, having never spoken to a coloured person before. They insisted we joined them on the small stage and asked us to name our favourite songs. An hour or more of delight followed and neither of us have forgotten our meeting with the great star — Fats Waller. A footnote to this incident was that, much to my fascination, and that of the waiters, Fats and all his entourage had a large fillet steak topped with several fried eggs every day for their breakfast!

Peter joined me at the High School when he was old enough to go to the kindergarten — we both remember his first day there, which was a bit disastrous. On our arrival we had to hand in our health certificates to our respective form teachers, but Peter hadn't got his — either Ma had forgotten to give it to him or more likely he had lost

Fats Waller gave me his autograph when he stayed at the Grand

it. Poor little chap, he was not allowed to join all the juniors for assembly and was left all alone standing by the headmistress's desk at the bottom of the staircase. By the time assembly was over and I was walking upstairs with my class mates he was sitting on a teacher's lap, crying, so I was called over to pacify him, but to no avail — he yelled louder. I was extremely embarrassed and returned to my class. Presumably our parents were telephoned and eventually one of them arrived to sort it all out. Peter did then spend a year there, which he enjoyed, but neither of us have forgotten the event and still look at each other and say 'Parents!'

Some of my friends took packed lunches but I liked school dinners — probably because they were more suitable for children than the very rich and, to us, monotonous food on the hotel menus. My

favourite pudding looked rather like a crispy rock cake on the top —
softer underneath and full of currants and raisins, served with cus-
tard. I always had a good appetite but once this led to trouble. We
ate in the dining room in the school basement and had to stand
behind our chairs waiting for all the teachers to arrive and say grace.
On this particular occasion we were still standing waiting and soup
had already been served into soup plates on the table in front of us. I
could not resist having a spoonful whilst still standing. Unfortunately
some of my friends began to giggle and so did I. This caused tomato
soup to spurt down out of my nose. As you can imagine, giggles
spread and I was sent out of the dining room with no lunch, still
hungry!

On my way home from school I passed a dairy at the top of
Regency Square. I can still see the tiled walls with pictures of cows
and green fields and even smell the little currant buns they sold, two
for 1d. These meant far more to Peter and me than the very rich
cakes being pushed around the hotel lounge on trolleys. Our
favourite supper was chicken sandwiches and tinned pineapple,
normally brought in by the floor waiter, a young man called Tommy
Blaine. He worked in the hotel for a number of years, returning after
the war to a more senior position in the main dining room. Peter and
I, like most children, had a cruel streak and teased him about his
smelly feet!

When we had a cookery lesson at school, we were expected to
take our own ingredients. Life was made very easy for me because I
would hand the list of the required ingredients to my mother who
would telephone down to the kitchen and read it out. A little while
later, Tommy would bring it all up to our sitting room on a silver tray
with each ingredient weighed and neatly wrapped in greaseproof
paper.

Living in the hotel, the routine of my school days began when I
was woken by the chambermaid with a cup of tea. I then washed
and dressed and went into my parents' bedroom to say good morning.
After that it was downstairs in the lift to have a solitary breakfast in
the main dining room at our special table on the right of the double

doors. There were not many guests about before 9 a.m. but my waiter friends made sure I was well fed before leaving. My favourite breakfast was kidneys, bacon and tomatoes — heaven — the one meal that I did dream about during the war years when I was really hungry.

After breakfast I would cross the seafront road (accompanied by a page boy if I was still small enough not to go across alone), and I would wait for the bus to come. One day another girl was standing there also waiting for the bus and said, 'Are you waiting for the bus?' When I replied, 'Yes, are you?' she asked, 'Do you go to the High School?' Margaret Lloyd soon become a very close friend and we often laughed when we recalled this very intelligent conversation because we were both wearing our green High School uniforms!

In my Brighton and Hove High School uniform when I was about 14

6

Christmas Time

Christmas during my childhood was different to the very commercial celebrations of today. Generally most people would decorate their home with a small Christmas tree. Not everyone could afford turkey, however — many had goose, which was smaller, or just a chicken — both very much a treat.

In the Grand it was of course very special, and began with the arrival of a huge Christmas tree. It came in the middle of the night (when all the guests had gone to their rooms) on a large lorry with all the branches tied up with rope so it could pass through the wide-opened revolving door. It was then dragged through the main hall and placed in a large container at the base of the stairwell — it was so tall it reached up to the third floor. Getting the tree in place was both difficult and painful for the porters and other staff, scratching their hands and arms on sharp pine needles.

When Peter and I went downstairs to have our breakfast the next morning a lovely scent of pine wafted all the way up the stairwell and we ran down the staircase rather than use the lift so we could see and smell it all the way down from every level. All the pine needles that must have been shed on its journey across the thick Turkish carpet would have been removed by then and the decorating had begun. This was done by the ladies from the offices, who used long poles to place the baubles on the branches they could not otherwise reach, with page boys going up ladders to help. The silver star on the very top had to be put on before the tree was hoisted into position. By mid-morning it was complete and the effect was glorious. Lots of lovely silver tinsel was draped across each branch, large colourful glass baubles hung everywhere and fairy lights glittered over the whole tree. Most of the guests who came to stay for Christmas had not yet arrived and for a few days the tree seemed to be the very best bit of Christmas — a small miracle — even overshadowing the excitement of presents and parties to come.

I suppose I would have been ten or eleven years old when, one year, a few weeks before Christmas, Pa took me in his car to London to buy toys for the children who came to the Christmas parties at the Grand. Of course for me this was rather special. I was allowed to help choose games, jigsaws and books and then we went for lunch at a very special restaurant called Frascati's. Because the manager there was a friend of Pa, we were both made a fuss of by the waiters as well as having the most scrumptious lunch.

On Christmas Eve we had to go to bed early — mind you, it seemed we had to do so far too often — especially in the summer when the sun was still shining on the sea and we could see people swimming. But on Christmas Eve we went to bed willingly — even if we couldn't sleep. I was always still wide awake when Ma came up after dinner later in the evening and began to pack pillow cases with our presents. We never had stockings because she put all the family presents which had come by post into the pillow cases — still wrapped with brown paper and string. Ma's and Pa's gifts would be in white tissue paper — no Sellotape in those days, only elastic bands and string. I could always hear the rustling of paper and other mysterious sounds as this was done on the old oak chest that stood in the corridor outside my bedroom and it was hard to pretend I was asleep!

Many of the regular guests, who became family friends over the years, were very generous to us. In particular, I remember a large shiny black paint box gave me great joy — and as I got older I was also given several pretty little evening purses, some decorated with beads and embroidery. I still have some of the books which were given to me then by the hotel accountant who came down from London regularly to work with my father. These included annuals full of coloured pictures and, as I got older, fine leather-bound copies of Shakespeare and various poets.

On one occasion I was given a fairy doll fixed in a very large box surrounded by fairyland decorations. I clearly recall that, at the time, my father said that I had too many presents and that my fairy doll must be taken to the children's hospital. This we did after Christmas and I don't remember being very upset as I didn't particularly like dolls. From then on every November, Peter and I would have a sort out of toys and books and I well remember that we had to check that every piece of each jigsaw puzzle was in the correct box. In early December this would be followed by a trip with Ma to deliver them to the children's hospital.

Christmas Day began by waking early to see if Father Christmas had been — seeing if the bulging white pillow cases with a cracker at the top were waiting on the floor beside our beds. Then to church for the carol service and back home to the hotel for Christmas Day lunch. In the early years we always went to the large Christmas party in the ballroom in the afternoon. Needless to say, the decorations were spectacular and included another Christmas tree which was completely bedecked with presents. Games like musical chairs followed, with the small hotel dance band playing in the background, and then we had an entertainer — either a Punch and Judy Show or a conjuror. The party ended with all the hundred or so children gathered round the tree to receive their presents. There were several other large parties for children before and after Christmas which were given by residents and the tickets sold in aid of charities.

My close friend Margaret Lloyd would be invited, which made it all the more fun. I have to admit, however, by the time she and I reached our early teens we found it rather boring, endeavouring to disappear during what we now considered childish games, and only returning for the tea and presents! The Boxing Day fancy dress party was probably the most exciting, when we would be taken to a shop near the Theatre Royal which hired out costumes. I can see myself now, dressed as a French artist in long black and baggy silk trousers, a coloured smock and a large black floppy satin beret, holding a wooden palette. I never won a prize but I loved the dressing up!

As we got older we had Christmas dinner in the evening with our parents and I can still remember the large cotton-wool snowballs (with paper hats and presents inside) on all the tables instead of crackers which everyone would throw across the dining room. By this time I must have become slightly flirtatious as my speciality was to throw one towards a young and very handsome Kenneth Newton, who sat at a table near ours with his parents and grandparents ... More about this particular young man later.

During the school week Margaret lived with her three aunts who ran a nursing home next door to the Grand. On Friday evenings she returned by bus to her home in Midhurst in West Sussex where her father was vicar. Her mother was a rather strict, large and grumpy lady — hardly surprising that she was grumpy, as the Reverend Lloyd had a reputation for falling off his bicycle when he'd had a few drinks! I would often go home with Margaret for the weekend — it wasn't very exciting except for Sundays, when we had to go to church three times. At least it was exciting for Margaret, because if she was lucky, she would be able to gaze at Percy, the choirboy to whom she was passionately devoted for a while!

Later Margaret often came and spent the night with us, particularly when Peter was still quite a little boy. She was two years older than me, therefore six years older than Peter and because she came from a clergy family, my parents considered her sensible and responsible and, if they were going out (usually to the Theatre Royal), she was left in charge. Margaret had a rather serious demeanour but this was misleading as she was quite the most mischievous person I knew and had the most wicked giggle — but she could be very bossy. During the war she achieved a high rank as a young major in the ATS (the Auxilliary Terratorial Service — a forerunner of the Women's Royal Army Corps). On one particular occasion she sent Peter off to have his bath — he always complained that she scrubbed his back too hard — and then it was my turn, after which it was Margaret's turn.

But she returned from the bathroom very angry, saying I had not cleaned the bath ready for her. I well remember trying to explain that it was the chambermaid who cleaned the bath. But she was furious, took me back into the bathroom and made me do it. The trouble was, I had no idea how, so most of the bath was clean by the time Margaret had demonstrated how it was done. Oh happy days!

7

Social Awakenings and Royalty

The walk home to the hotel from school left an impression on me, which has stayed to this day. Leaving the High School, at the top of Montpelier Road, I walked down the hill towards the sea. I would turn left into Western Road until I reached the turning into Clarence Square, then into Regency Square and from there a short walk brought me to a small newsagent's shop on a corner where I turned right into a cobbled street, lined either side with continuous rows of mews cottages. These had been built to accommodate the horses and carriages, with rooms above for the stable men. By this time, they were mainly used as workshops in which cars were repaired and families lived in cheap rooms above — no electricity or running water, only outside taps. Children would be playing outside on the cobblestones and many had no shoes. Their mothers were sitting at the bottom of the staircases, gossiping. These surroundings gave an impression of poverty and neglect.

At the lower end, where the cobbles became tarmac, I walked through the Grand Hotel garage past large cars, including several Rolls-Royces, to the back-door entrance into the hotel; down a short length of wide, white marble steps with highly polished brass handrails either side; through the two sets of wide heavy double doors into the hotel corridor; and stepped onto a thick-piled Turkish carpet — immediately becoming aware of warmth and luxury. From there I went on in, past the lift and into the hotel lounge where Ma would be sitting in an armchair having tea with several lady residents. Nearby was a large trolley with masses of rich creamy cakes such as gâteaux, chocolate éclairs and pastries. Because I was only a child I was obviously unaware at the time of the deep impression all this had on me, but I have always felt strongly that it was very wrong that some people should have so much and others so very little.

As the hotel manager's family we were neither kith nor kin. We had a very unsettled and strange position — we didn't really 'belong' to either group — staff or guests. This was illustrated when another of my ambitions was thwarted. I was about fourteen and I wanted to join the Girl Guides who met in the church hall of St Margaret's Church just around the corner in Cannon Place. I was told very firmly by Pa that I could not do so, because several of the waiters had daughters there and it would not have been 'proper' for me to join them.

Ma must have been aware of this rather odd existence but she was a very kind, gentle and loving soul, devoted to Pa, whom she did her utmost to support. I know that she was aware how lonely many of the women residents living in the hotel were (in spite of most of them being very wealthy widows), but it cannot have been easy for her having so little in common. I know that most of the staff adored her; she was always kind and sympathetic to their problems. But in later years, after Pa's death, she seldom spoke of her life in the Grand and if ever I suggested that I took her back there perhaps for tea, she never ever wanted to go. To my knowledge, she never went into the hotel again after my father retired.

After our parents had gone downstairs to dinner and I was in bed, some of the chambermaids who worked on the seventh floor would come and chat to me in my bedroom. One in particular told me hair-raising stories about the First World War, which had only ended five years before I was born. She and many others had horrific memories of those terrible years. At weekends during fine weather large groups of men, all wearing the same bright blue trousers and jackets with red ties, were brought by charabancs from the St Dunstan's Convalescent Home at Ovingdean to walk along the seafront. Many were blind and they walked arm-in-arm with their carers. Others were pushed in wheelchairs, many of them had no legs, and others who were very disabled by horrendous war wounds were pushed along on stretchers.

Even as a young child the war stories and the sight of these men in blue upset me very much.

At other times we saw elderly ladies and gentlemen being pushed along in bath chairs — these were special chairs for invalids, and a line of them were parked opposite the Grand waiting to be hired. The chairs were large, all black with three wheels and a hood in case in rained, and they were pushed along by men who charged for their service.

Much has changed since we lived in the hotel as children during the thirties. At that time it was a world apart — almost a microcosm of British society. Many guests were titled and wealthy and others were the stars of the stage and screen who stayed there whilst performing at the Brighton theatres — the Theatre Royal and the Hippodrome. Several guests travelled on the fast London and Brighton trains, returning late evening and going back to London the following day for the evening performances. Our daily lives were naturally closer to the hotel staff, many of whom became our friends. Some lived in, and they all worked very hard for long hours and were not well paid. The front-of-house staff — those were the staff that had regular contact with the guests — were obliged to rely on gratuities — tips. Most guests were generous particularly at Christmas and Easter. This was in some ways and still is an iniquitous system, which the industry has tried to alter.

At all the large hotels the very senior staff who were in positions of considerable authority would prefer to pay the hotel company to employ them because the tips received were much greater than any wage. These included the head commissionaire, who was the first to greet arrivals, opening their car doors and organising porters to take their luggage to their rooms, and also the head waiter, who ensured guests sat at the table of their choice in the large dining room. The younger and less experienced staff were at a disadvantage to their

45

more senior colleagues, who knew the regular visitors quite well and who made a point of being somewhat subservient, but of course always very polite and helpful. When hotels introduced the 'tronc' system — a pooling of all tips which were then distributed by a percentage to all staff — it was not popular. Nor was the system of adding a percentage to guest accounts, as in each case the senior staff lost out and hotel guests preferred the more personal method of direct tipping at the end of their stay, or weekly tipping by the permanent guests.

The Prince of Wales — later King Edward (but who remained uncrowned and then became the Duke of Windsor) — came to lunch several times. However, like all the royal family, he never carried any ready cash so there were no tips — rather sad, as even a small recognition of the service he received would have been special and very much treasured by the staff. But that was how it was in those days. I doubt whether this has changed today — I would be surprised if the Queen carries any cash!

The staff — from the page boys up to the head porter and the commissionaire, the kitchen workers to the head chef, the commis waiter to the head waiter and the cleaners and chambermaids up to the head housekeeper — all were the backbone of the entire structure. Mother repeatedly told us that we must show great respect for the staff and explained that without their hard work the hotel could not function. After Christmas, in early January, a staff ball was held for them. This was an important occasion and when I was in my teens I recall Mother asking me which of my two long evening dresses I was planning to wear. Later I told her which one. She replied, 'No not that one, for the staff you should wear your newest and best,' and added that I should be sure to dance with everyone who asked me, including the page boys — because I was the manager's daughter! I didn't much like these young men, who always teased me.

I suppose I had several long evening dresses by the time I was 15, which may sound expensive and exciting, but it was not like that. Nearly all my clothes and my mother's were made by a local dressmaker called Miss Cuckoo. We had to go to her flat at the back of Brighton for fittings — probably it was cheaper for us to do this than for her to visit us. I took no pleasure in these visits — the overcrowded room she worked in smelled of stale cooking — cabbage in particular — and the dresses were awful, very 'little girlish' with puff sleeves and frills.

Among the staff, my best friends were George Stenning, the hotel upholsterer who was responsible for all the soft furnishings, and a Miss Plummer, the hotel telephonist who operated the old-fashioned switchboard. George had a huge workroom in the basement below the banqueting room which was filled with mattresses, cushions, pillows, eiderdowns, curtains, armchairs and lots of rolls of carpet and fabric all waiting to be made up or repaired.

When we first discovered George in his workroom, Peter and I had great fun jumping on and off and rolling about on all those things. Later when I had a craze of designing and making toy theatres with the help of 'Woody' the resident carpenter, George would find me beautiful offcuts to use for the curtains and help me to make things. There was also a nice man called Bill Pratt who was the hotel electrician and he did wonderful lighting effects for the stages in my theatres.

In those days there was no familiarity between children and adults and we did not know many of the staff members' Christian names unless we heard them addressed by my father as 'George' or 'Bill'. To Peter and me, it was always 'Mr Stenning' and 'Mr Pratt' and all the staff called us 'Master Peter' and 'Miss Pam' — perhaps this accounts for my dislike of being called by my Christian name other than by close friends. Today I still prefer 'Mrs Wilson' or 'Lady Newton', or even 'Mrs Newton'!

In 1933, when I was ten years old, there was great excitement and curiosity when a large Indian royal family came for a long visit. They included the young Prince and Princess of Khairpur State in India who were awaiting the birth of their first child. The prince's father, His Highness, the Mir of Khairpur State, made arrangements for several of the prince's sisters to attend St Mary's Hall School for Girls

47

in Kemp Town. It had been decided sea air would be beneficial, so they also bought a large house in Lewes Crescent.

Whilst living in the Grand, the Indian royal family occupied the whole of the first floor with several of their Indian servants, who served all their meals to them in their own rooms. I don't think they ever ate in the hotel dining room except at Christmas. Whenever they were seen in public the princess, her mother and the prince's mother were dressed in very beautiful saris, but the prince and the sisters dressed in English fashion, no doubt to help the girls to become accustomed to our ways in preparation for the time they would spend at their English school.

During the family's long stay in the Grand the new Indian prince was born, causing great joy to the whole family and, as reported in the national and local press, all the inhabitants of Khairpur State. My father was photographed congratualating the Indian prince on the front steps of the hotel with Directors of Spiers and Ponds. This was only the second birth to occur in the hotel — my arrival being the first. Among the other celebrations, the one I remember best was a very special fireworks display which took place from the ends of both the Palace Pier and West Pier (they didn't have fireworks when I was born as far as I know!). I was told by Mother to dress in my best — and only — party frock because she and I were going to go down to see the new baby. I was also taught how to curtsy to the princess, who was the equivalent of an English princess in her own right. When we entered their sitting room — a large room facing the sea — the princess was sitting in an armchair near the window. She was a very small dark lady, who seemed very shy but she did praise my curtsy, which was kind.

The baby was in a large, draped cot and, whilst Mother talked to the princess, I gazed at this rather curious very small infant, who I later described to my school friends as looking like a squashed prune!

A rather extraordinary addition to this story was that the baby, when aged just nine months, survived being accidentally shot by his father, who was suffering from a delirious fever. Apparently, the

The second baby to be born at the Grand! The *Evening Standard* was the first to print a picture of the newborn heir to the throne of Khairpur.

My father (far left) congratulates the Indian prince on the birth of his son

bullet went through his stomach and lung, exiting through his shoulder, but he did go on to succeed his father, becoming the new Mir of Khairpur in 1947. A very fortunate end to the story!

When the Indian family eventually left to go to live in their large house in Lewes Crescent I was often invited to children's parties there. These were rather special — lots of lovely food and presents, but best was playing games in the large enclosed gardens in the centre of the crescent — it always seemed to be summer and I suppose I was quite envious that the girls had these special gardens to play in. Living in the Grand, the nearest Peter and I got to having a garden was our beach hut by the West Pier. The huts were made half of wood and half of canvas and we used to have to put the canvas top on.

8

Brighton Beach, Heydays and Holidays

Before the Second World War, there were many pleasure boats on Brighton beach, taking holiday makers for trips round the piers. These large, heavy boats stayed all year round on the beaches and were hauled up and down over the pebbles on railway sleepers according to the seasons and the tides. During the summer season they were anchored in the sea and there was a ladder from the pebbles going up the stern end for passengers to climb aboard. One of the several boatmen would stand on the stern to help them up, at the same time shouting, 'Any more for the Skylark?' — a cry which Peter, then a small boy of five or six, imitated all day long until he too was allowed to stand on the boat and shout, much to the amusement of friends and family sitting outside the beach huts. He naturally was given plenty of free trips, to his delight.

We both learnt to swim quite young. I was taught by the corporation boatman, who would tow me behind his rowing boat by a rope, tied round my chest. Ma paid him 6d. (about 2½ pence) a lesson. His real job was to make sure all the people who were in the sea — most who could not swim — were safe, particularly at high tide when the beach was quite dangerous, as the pebbles formed deep shelves. Nothing could keep me out of the water after that, and later I joined the West Pier swimming club.

During the school summer holidays we spent all day down at our hut on the beach, taking picnic lunches and teas down with us. A particular highlight was when Pa bought Peter and me a canoe. Not like modern canoes, this was rather solid and heavy and very second-hand. At the time, the seventh-floor rooms were looked after by a young Russian chambermaid who suggested the name 'Rusalka' (Russian for mermaid) for the canoe, so this was duly painted on its side. There was an unfortunate accident when I was trying to steer *Rusalka* back on the beach at high tide. The sea was quite rough and the beach crowded, as I came in on a wave, a little girl stepped in front of the boat and was knocked over. Although I remember her yelling, she was not hurt, but I was very upset.

There was always a band on the east side of the West Pier. Mother and one or two friends from the hotel would sit in deckchairs and listen to them while doing their knitting. People used to stroll along the pier in the evening but had to pay. There was a theatre and a restaurant. One of the circular kiosks on the west side of the far end of the pier was a newspaper shop. I would save up my pennies to buy a weekly story magazine from the old man who used to keep them for me. There were entertainments on the far end of the pier on the semi-circular fishing jetties. Men used to ride bicycles and jump off the platform into the sea wearing flaming lifebelts and all sorts of peculiar things! It didn't really appeal to me. I enjoyed sitting on the seats with a wrought-iron back which lined both sides of the pier and gazing down at the sea.

Brighton seafront was always nearly empty of cars, except during the summer and bank holidays. There were a lot of buses around. When I went to school in the morning, walking over to the sea side of the road to catch the bus, there were very few people on it and hardly any cars around. Trolley buses used to run from Pool Valley to the top of Ditchling Road and there were a few trams.

When I was a child, people did not go away on holidays very often and going abroad was expensive. I do, however, have a clear picture of a brief holiday in St Margaret's Bay near Broadstairs on the Kent coast. I was about 5 years old and we all went by train and stayed in a boarding house on the sea front. When we had been shown into the room where we would all sleep, Ma became very upset as there was

Sitting on the canoe *Rusalka* with my best friend Margie (on left) during the year we tried for School Certificate – we should have been studying!

no cot for Peter, still a baby, and Pa pulled out a large drawer from a chest of drawers into which Peter was put and all was well. The sandy beach was wonderful after all the pebbles at Brighton.

I have many happy memories of early childhood spent with Auntie Dor-Dor, my mother's eldest sister, Uncle Marcel (who was a French artist), and their daughter June when I went to stay with them in their pretty little house on Barnes Common near Richmond. My cousin June and I were good pals as little girls, though sadly we did not see much of each other as adults. The walls of the house were covered with my Uncle Marcel's pictures — he was a fine water-colourist and became a much-respected interior designer, known especially for his work in the big liners of the time, including the *Mauritania* and the ill-fated *Lusitania*. I still have a photograph of his design for the ballroom of the Glen Eagles Hotel when it was first built.

During holidays spent at Barnes we would all walk together on the common with Podger, their much-loved dog of mixed origins. If it was too wet to walk, Auntie Dor-Dor (who always had a special treat in store for June and me) allowed us to rummage through the dressing-up chest in her bedroom, which contained a number of her evening dresses. Most of these had a tale to tell, as she had worn them to the balls celebrating the opening of the ballrooms on the great ocean liners in the 1920s. Cousin June and I had enormous fun pretending to be grand ladies of society.

Holidays changed when cars came on the scene. When I was ten years old and Peter was six we went to stay in Piltdown, near Uckfield in Sussex. Pa took us in a taxi, but then went back to Brighton as he had to work. It was a very hot summer and I didn't like leaving the sea. We stayed in a house which was a tea place and slept in an attic bedroom which was small and hot. We visited a farm nearby because Peter liked watching the cows being milked. I remember sitting on the wall by Piltdown Pond and fishing for tad-poles with a piece of string and a jam jar, but I never caught anything.

In 1935 my father acquired his first car, which was a brown Austin

Seven, and we drove to North Wales. It was a very long way and Peter and I were both travel sick in this very small car. I remember the rushing torrents of the waterfalls at Betws-y-Coed and seeing the Welsh mountains. I know that neither Peter nor I, nor my mother, liked the continuous driving and we wanted to go home. We had a much better holiday the next year when I was 13 and we stayed with Ma in a bungalow in East Wittering in Sussex, but again Pa had to stay and work at the Grand, so could only join us from time to time. We met up with other friends from Brighton and spent all of our time on the beach, with occasional walks to the village shop.

Pa bought his second car in 1937 and this had a semi-soft top. He insisted on taking us to Switzerland in it, but Mother wasn't keen. I was about fourteen and had to sit in the back, feeling queasy. We reached Ostend and drove through Belgium, inadvertently crossing the Maginot Line, which was built to stop the Germans from invading France — but it didn't! Father didn't realise what it was until we were half-way across. It was all rather scary because although the countryside looked quite normal, underground there were all kinds of secret tunnels and defences and lots of French soldiers about. Pa panicked when a large, fierce Alsatian appeared out of nowhere. He promptly wound up the window and sped off. We reached Switzerland via France and stayed in a hotel by Lake Lucerne with wonderful views of the mountains and where I proceeded to develop appendicitis. The traditional Swiss treatment did not involve an operation, but instead a nurse applied boiling hot camomile compresses to my stomach. When I returned to Britain, the family doctor was furious and said my appendix should have been removed, though in the end it never was.

Father was very fed up because my illness had prevented our progress and he was desperate to leave, so after a week I was packed into the back of the car again. Between the lakes Lucerne and Lausanne we stopped at a place with beautiful views and both Mother and I wanted to stay there, but Father was determined to press on. Mother suffered in silence. Montreux was lovely and we saw the Jungfrau mountain. We came back via Paris and as we were walking down the Champs-Elysées I met up with a school friend who lived just outside the city and we had a coffee to celebrate. I also remember seeing a little blue suede handbag in the Galeries Lafayette that I desperately wanted, but Father said we didn't have enough money. It was the only thing I ever wanted really badly, but as a child I didn't often get what I desired because our parents were afraid of spoiling us.

Ma was not robustly healthy, as a result of her sickly childhood, and did not enjoy travelling. Father, on the other hand, was always restless and had to be on the go. Thus as we got older he expected either Peter or me to accompany him when he went away either in this country or abroad. In the early days of owning a car he took me to Scarborough in Yorkshire where we stayed in another Grand Hotel, which also belonged to Spiers and Ponds. It was cold, wet and windy and my *single* bedroom was so large you could have put six beds in it, with a vast window facing the bleak, grey North Sea.

9

Strikes, Gangsters, Celebrities

Father was a complex character, much admired and respected in the hotel industry both in Brighton and London by staff and guests and by various executives in large hotel groups throughout the country. There must have been moments when he was aware and puzzled by the extreme comparisons of the surrounding wealth and opulence and the manner in which his stepmother and stepsister lived in Derby. He loved and enjoyed his work and he certainly admired anybody, either staff or guests, who worked hard, honestly and successfully. The staff considered him a very fair employer but a somewhat hard man in certain circumstances. I have a book called *Imperial Place* by Arnold Bennett — a story of an entrepreneur in the hotel world called Evelyn. It was given to my father by Sir Harry Preston, owner of the Queen's Hotel Brighton, Mayor of Brighton and a close friend and admirer. In it he has written 'To another Evelyn, with sincere gratitude for kindness and help during Christmas, March 1931'.

I have come to believe that Pa's somewhat severe manner was caused by a lack of security concerning his job. During the 1920s and 1930s good positions were hard to come by and many hoteliers obtained their positions by being 'who they were' and 'knowing the right people'. He had none of these advantages when he began as Secretary to the Grand Hotel Company (before it became part of the Spiers and Ponds Group). His crowning achievement came in 1947 when he was made General Managing Director of the whole Spiers and Ponds Group, which owned about a dozen hotels in the south of England.

But there was another side to him, particularly when he performed his famous trick of balancing an (empty?) champagne bottle on his very bald head. He then did a kind of limbo dance movement, going down backwards to lie flat on the floor; he then repeated the movement until he was standing upright again. Quite a remarkable performance and the bottle never fell off!

One of the more exciting events that took place was when all the kitchen staff went on strike — probably during the early 1930s. At that time there were a number of foreigners working there and certainly the conditions were not good — very hot and noisy, crowded and uncomfortable. Father was already dressed in black tailcoat and and pin-striped trousers in preparation for a large banquet that evening. As soon as he was told that there was trouble, he went down to the kitchens and tried to speak to the men — about 30 or 40 of them, some of whom threatened him with knives. Many probably did not understand him. He then took off his black tailcoat, rolled up his sleeves, put on a large apron and went over to the sinks and began to wash the large heavy black pots and pans. The loyal, local British men began to clap and cheer, and within minutes all the men joined in and order was restored — the evening's work proceeding normally. The police who had been alerted left and a successful banquet followed. This became known as the Bolshevik strike and was often referred to with pride by the hotel staff, all of whom certainly admired Pa's courage.

Although I was not present when this happened, it is not difficult for me to imagine because I knew the vast kitchens well. Peter and I often wandered down there to see what was going on, especially if we knew there was to be a banquet or large dinner that evening, because we knew exactly where the silver plates of petits fours would be. These were sweetmeats of all kinds to be served at the end of a meal, and our wicked childish fingers always managed to put several of these in our mouths and pockets. No one seemed to mind — or maybe no one ever guessed!

Father was an excellent raconteur and had numerous stories of the colourful events which occurred during his years of management at the Grand. One particular story that I remember was when Father's cool head averted a very unpleasant and explosive situation on a night when the London race gangs visited and sparks flew with the resident Brighton race gangs. During the mid-1930s the annual Brighton Race Week was a time when the town was accustomed to considerable disturbance. This came mainly from Londoners who came for the races, amongst whom there were always rowdy groups of men — many of them criminals and well known to the police. They would descend on the town centre from the race course for an evening of heavy drinking and always caused trouble.

On one particular evening following a day's racing, several of these unwelcome individuals came into the hotel, sat down in the hall and ordered drinks. To begin with all was well, but the more they drank the more cantankerous and belligerent they became. Father had already contacted the police, who were patrolling the town in case of trouble. It was getting late and nearing closing time for the bars, when a second race gang arrived and walked into the hotel hall. When these men saw the first group sitting drinking the two gangs began exchanging insults, at which point one of the new arrivals very deliberately wiped his muddy boots on an overcoat owned by a member of the first gang which was slung over the back of his chair. Strong words and threats were exchanged and knives produced. Father, who had been keeping an eye on them all, tried to intervene and calm them down but was pushed to one side. The hall porter had also already alerted the police who, expecting trouble, had been waiting outside on the seafront and much to my father's relief, appeared in the hotel foyer at this precise moment. All of the terrified guests and most of the staff had already moved well away, out of the hall. Even though the police were outnumbered by the two gangs, they took control, handcuffed the majority and marched them out to waiting police vans. Much as my father disliked the publicity caused by this event, he was obliged to give evidence in court.

An incident which followed soon after when I was about thirteen demonstrates the attitudes of that time which were so different to those of today. My father had become a good friend of the Chief of Police, and both families knew each other quite well as we had adjacent huts on the beach. Jean, the daughter, was in the same class as me at the High School and I had become a little friendly with her elder brother, Trevor, who was in the sixth form at the grammar school. I remember going to see a performance of Gilbert and Sullivan's *The Mikado* in which he took the leading role. On a later occasion when I was alone in the beach hut changing into my swimsuit, Trevor entered the hut and before I could avoid it, he gave me a sloppy French kiss! I was surprised and indignant because I had not encouraged him and instinctively slapped him hard on the face. Almost immediately my parents arrived and, realising something was amiss, my father demanded to know what had happened. Embarrassed, I tried to explain but Pa's reaction was to blame me entirely because I believe he was anxious not to offend his colleague, Trevor's father. I was told to apologise and banished to my room in the hotel. It seemed very unfair to me at the time, but in hindsight possibly understandable, that my father's foremost concern was to retain his good relationship with the Chief of Police.

A very similar event occurred a few years later when I was seventeen, with a twenty-one-year-old Kenneth Newton, who was to become my second husband.

As I have explained previously, the Grand was regularly visited by celebrities who came to perform in the Brighton theatres. One of the most striking was Tom Mix, a famous American film star, who came *into* the Grand with his horse! On his arrival he would not leave the horse outside, and insisted that the Head Porter (a nice gentle and kind man named Albert Williams) open up the double revolving doors. Tom Mix then led the horse up the outside steps, through the doors and into the hall. Father was telephoned and rushed down to sort this extraordinary situation out. I followed Pa and sat on the stairs just above, where I could see immediately below me a large white horse, with reins and saddle of bright scarlet, being held by a small man wearing white jodhpurs, riding boots, a white suit covered in red sequins and a large white Stetson hat — a very glamorous cowboy and altogether a wonderful sight.

During a long and intense discussion between Father and the cowboy, the horse behaved impeccably and staff and guests alike gathered round to watch. Meanwhile Albert hurried out to Artillery Street where he was able to arrange a stable. Following much argument, Tom Mix took the horse out and round to see the stables and reluctantly agreed that the horse could stay there, while he was staying in a room on the first floor. Everybody was very relieved — especially Pa — and Tom Mix and his horse were both treated as honoured guests whilst performing at the Hippodrome for the week. Tom Mix was allowed to ride his horse along the seafront each morning, which was of course very good publicity for his show.

Pa was frequently given free seats by the managers of cinemas and theatres, for his own use or to give to guests or staff. Consequently, Peter and I were often sent off to see films on our own, particularly to the Palladium cinema, which in those days was next door to the Grand. This was probably because there was very little space for us to play in within our rooms on the seventh floor and Ma could not keep her eye on us, when we (frequently) wandered off to explore all over the vast building we called home.

Max Miller, the famous comedian who performed in several Royal Command Performances, frequently visited the hotel. On one occasion Pa was given free seats by him for a matinée at the Hippodrome. Peter and I were sometimes given the chance to use these if the show was considered suitable by our parents. I don't think Ma and Pa could have ever seen Max Miller's shows because they couldn't have been less suitable. The seats we were given were usually in the front row of the stalls — probably because being so close gave one a stiff neck, looking up at the stage! I was about twelve or thirteen and whilst I did not understand many of the jokes, I sensed by the audience's response that they were very risqué and rude! So during the interval I took my brother home and tried to explain that the show was unsuitable for him!

My somewhat puritanical attitude must have been as a result of Ma telling us, prior to all our visits to the cinema, that if parts of the film were what we knew would not meet with her approval, we should put our heads *under* the seats!

Among the many famous people of the time who stayed in the hotel and whose autographs Mr Pozzi, the Head Waiter, obtained for me, there was George Arliss — an elderly American star of many films. Also Harry Lauder — elderly, but still very popular in British music hall for his singing and jokes in a broad Scottish accent. Then there was another odd American called Jimmy Durante, a popular comedian who always seemed to be shouting and, due to having a very large nose, was known as 'Snozzel' Durante.

Jean Batten was not a film star, but a highly acclaimed aviatrix from New Zealand who came in 1935 for a long rest after touring both England and the USA. Known as 'Garbo of the Skies', she was the first pilot to fly solo from England to Australia and back again in 1934.

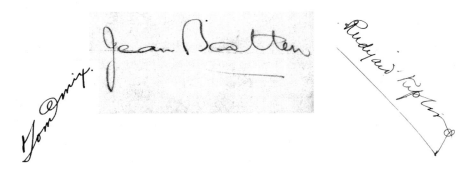

The Head Waiter helped me to collect autographs of some of the film stars, musicians, writers and adventurers who stayed at the Grand

Richard Tauber, the opera singer, was a regular visitor whilst singing at Covent Garden, and who told Pa the sea air helped his voice! It probably helped to expand his lungs; I recently confessed to my doctor that I was still smoking (at 85) and have always believed that my lungs may have stayed healthy because Ma put me out in my pram, on the balcony of the sixth-floor bedroom where I was born, in mid-January. My current doctor roared with laughter, saying it was the best explanation he had heard yet!

Held in awe by Pa, staff and guests was the great writer Rudyard Kipling. A regular visitor, he always had the same room, and as I recall from my child's perspective, he was rather a scary sort of man with lots of whiskers!

I had a personal encounter with Sir Anthony Eden, who succeeded Winston Churchill as Prime Minister in 1955. He and other ministers were staying in the hotel for the Conservative Party Conference in 1937. It was a sunny day and I was standing on the hotel steps outside the main entrance selling Queen Alexandra roses on Rose Day, when this tall handsome man jumped from a large black car and rushed past me up the steps. As he did so, he knocked over the tray of roses, which was held by a ribbon around my neck, and all the pink flower emblems flew out of the tray, over the steps and onto the pavement. He apologised profusely and insisted on helping me and a page boy pick them all up. I had no idea who he was until I was told later by the hall porter.

One of Pa's later stories was about Fanny and Johnnie Cradock, who starred in the first television show about cookery. Prior to this they had written a cookery column for the *Daily Telegraph*. They came to stay in the Grand during a busy high season weekend without booking and to their annoyance had to be given a bedroom at the back, not overlooking the sea. No one knew who they were but they were treated with the same consideration and courtesy as all guests. A couple of weeks later, an article by Fanny Cradock appeared in the *Daily Telegraph*, full of outrageous comments and criticisms of the hotel, complaining about the food and their room, saying they had been woken by the clattering of dustbin lids during the night. Pa was furious and threatened to sue them, but in the end he wrote to them saying the remarks were exaggerated and untrue, but in an endeavour to pacify them, offered them a night in a seafront room at a very reduced rate, but they did not have the courtesy to reply. The staff concerned were told to be quieter with the dustbins in the future!

I always remember seeing Fanny being interviewed on TV some years later when she said, 'I have always enjoyed being rude!'

10

Teenage Challenges and a Special Friendship

The constant reminders from Father to mind our manners with the guests and from Mother to be on our best behaviour with the staff have stayed with me throughout my life. But I don't regret being brought up in the Grand. I've had more experiences and challenges and seen more of life than I would have done otherwise. I wouldn't change any of it. I liked the excitement of living in a hotel, although really it was *too* stimulating and exciting for a child. I was interested in the people and the events. But my brother hated it. He became a farmer and got as far away from it as possible.

Mother, who was a piano teacher before she married, tried to teach me to play, but it was a disaster. I was also never athletic though I did excel at table tennis. Most of all I wanted to dance and when I was about eleven I started ice-skating lessons. The ice rink was just round the corner at the bottom of West Street and my friend Margie Miller and I used to go regularly on Saturday mornings. I didn't find it easy, though I took lessons. Just before the war, when I was about fourteen or fifteen, we were both in a Christmas Charity Ice Show when we danced to the 'Waltz of the Flowers' by Tchai-kovsky — me in pale mauve, Margie in bright red.

The rehearsals were great fun because we had a small group of followers — boys we knew who both teased and encouraged us (to fall over) from the far side of the barrier. Both of us were very wary of our respective fathers — Margie's father owned Courtlands Hotel in Hove and so they knew each other — and whilst we were not actually forbidden to be in the show, we knew neither of our fathers approved of the situation. As two old ladies of eighty-five, we still enjoy a good giggle remembering our brief moment of theatrical fame — though I think each of us was equally terrified, particularly of falling over and making idiots of ourselves.

In the Grand there was a young Canadian called Tony who worked as the gentlemen's cloakroom attendant. He was an ice hockey player and a good skater. How thrilled I was when he took me very, very fast round and round the ice rink, holding hands — arms crossed over, skating fashion — until on one occasion, going I'm sure too fast, we had to swerve to avoid another skater and ended up going head first over the barrier. Luckily neither of us was hurt but he was worried about my father finding out and him losing his job!

A blissful moment was being asked to dance the ten-step (the fastest dance on ice) by a young blond Swede who was appearing in the current ice show at the time. I shall never forget the thrill of the speed of the music and the confidence he must have had in order to keep me upright!

At about that time in 1938, Daphne Walker, the current junior ice dance champion (and who went on to win a bronze medal in the Prague World Championships, aged fourteen), was staying in the hotel and performing at the ice rink; she was a pretty girl not much older than me. As I left for the hotel for my Saturday session carrying my boots (white — special) and skates, two young boys came up and asked me for my autograph, which I willingly gave them! They had mistaken me for Daphne — the champion — very satisfying! It is strange how early pleasures remain — I still love waffles and maple syrup, which we had after every skating session, but now I have the maple syrup on porridge.

At this time I was still having problems at the High School, however, and Father went to see the headmistress who said something to the effect that I was very difficult and asked him to find somewhere else for me. I wasn't aware of being difficult, but I certainly wasn't happy. I think it was a mixture of reasons, including boredom and frustration due to the late identification of my poor eyesight.

I left school in the summer of 1939 at the age of sixteen and eventually Pa agreed to my attending the Brighton Art School. This was only on the condition, however, that I studied dress design rather than painting and drawing, as he thought this might have more of a commercial future. When I did eventually start at the Art School in the autumn, a lot of the girls of my age were wearing trousers, which was relatively new. When I announced that I was going to buy a pair, Pa insisted that if I did so, I would have to enter the Grand via the back entrance through the garages, as trousers were considered not quite *de rigueur*!

The head of the department was a Miss Early, a rather thin and fussy little lady, but a good teacher who taught us how to make our own paper dress patterns and hats. This was quite good fun, but I soon found that I was not missed when I went into the life classes! These were held in a large room where, surrounded by life-size stone statues, we stood at our easels and learned to draw and paint real-life nudes — men and women. I found that I was rather good at this and loved the atmosphere of silent concentration. One day this peace and quiet was interrupted by a crash, when the model, a, dreadfully emaciated young woman, collapsed in a dead faint across the plinth on which she was standing. It must have been a cold winter's day because the electric heaters which were built into the plinth were full on and she was badly burnt as she fell. I am afraid that I, and several of the other young women, found the incident exciting, as Don, the art master, a youngish, bearded individual, rushed over and carried her out into the restroom — all very romantic!

My very favourite guest who came to the Grand frequently was 'Mrs M' — May Marlow. By the time I knew her she was already a 'lady of a certain age' but as young at heart as one could ever wish to be. She had had a successful career in music hall before marrying Harry Marlow, secretary of the Royal Variety Artistes' Benevolent Fund and Institution. This was a charity which owned a large house in Richmond where elderly people connected with the theatre were cared for when they fell on hard times — there being no state pensions in those days. Mrs M's life had been full of ups and downs and she was a little woman who had had tuberculosis in her spine which had left her, sadly, rather hunchbacked. In spite of the age difference she was my greatest friend, confidante and support during my difficult teenage years.

With the delightful May Marlow and her husband, Harry, at an event in the Grand's ballroom

Most evenings my mother would sit in the main hall of the Grand Hotel drinking tea or coffee with several older lady residents, chatting and listening to the small orchestra playing in the background. On this particular evening, I must have been in one of my black moods, when Mrs M looked me straight in the eye and said, 'Let's pretend we are in a Lyons Corner House' (a large chain of very noisy cafeterias which served food all day, and where the waitresses were known as 'Nippys' because they nipped around so fast). Mrs M stood up, draped her scarf around her waist as a pretend apron, and picked up the very heavy silver tray loaded with silver teapots, cups, jugs and sugar bowls, and said, 'I'm a Nippy, I'm a Nippy.' She then proceeded to rattle the tray so loudly that the Tom Priddy Orchestra stopped playing, everyone stopped speaking, and the laughter was such that some had tears running down their faces! Even Pa, who at first wasn't that amused, eventually joined in the laughter and my black mood went in a flash.

On another occasion when the difficult teenager was again being moody, there was an even more hilarious incident. In order to make Saturday evenings a bit special for hotel guests the small orchestra was often accompanied by a vocalist. This time a small rotund gentleman, quite a good baritone, sang the 'Song of the Flea' which involved him rotating his head round and round singing, 'Ha, ha, ha, ha,' in time to the music.

Halfway through his performance, Mrs M sat up very straight in her chair, imitating his movements exactly in time to the music. Everybody began to giggle, and nothing would stop her. Even the waiters, porters and pages paused to watch. Finally the music stopped and the poor man had to stop singing. The laughter could have been heard at the end of the West Pier! My mood was gone and I shall never forget the sense of fun that filled everyone there. She was such a ray of sunshine.

I must have become somewhat inured to the very public and exposed life of living in a large hotel. I do not recall being at all embarrassed when returning home (most often from trips to the cinema) with various friends, both male and female, to be greeted at the main entrance, first by the hall porter, and then any other staff friends who happened to be around. We would then continue on into the main lounge or hall where Ma and Pa were having drinks with those guests who were also their friends.

After the war, when life had returned somewhat to normal, Mrs M's final 'bequest' to me was when I returned to the hotel one evening, having been out on a date with the young man who would eventually become my husband. Frank was introduced to her as she sat in the lounge with Ma and various other ladies. She looked him very straight in the eye and said with a twinkle, 'I hope your intentions are honourable?' Frank rose to the occasion beautifully and replied, 'But of course, Ma'am,' and kissed her hand, after which they became firm friends. She had always wanted to know all about my various boyfriends, but I never minded as she always enquired with such good humour. Sadly she died soon after Frank and I were married and I shall always wish I had known her for longer.

It was through May Marlow that I came to sell programmes at the Royal Command Performance at the London Palladium. Mrs M organised the programme sellers and invited me to join them — quite an honour, as the whole event was in aid of the Royal Variety Club and always attended by the royal family. We were somewhat handpicked, most girls being daughters of parents connected with the theatrical world. One who became quite a good friend was Sheila, daughter of the impresario Tom Arnold (famous for the ice shows). We were expected to wear our very best evening gowns and had to learn to curtsy. When the show was over, the programme sellers stood with the performers on either side of the wide staircase leading down to the theatre foyer and we all curtseyed or bowed as the royal family walked slowly down. On one such occasion I stood next to the comedian and actor Bob Hope. He was shaking like a leaf and kept asking me what to do. I tried to explain that if any of the royal family spoke to him, he had to bow — but he didn't understand what a bow was — being an American, the word was not in his vocabulary! Anyway, the King did stop, spoke to him and praised his performance. Poor Bob just about survived, afterwards thanking me very profusely for my help!

After another Royal Command Performance, I was standing on the stairs as the royal family passed by. First the King and Queen and Princess Elizabeth came down, followed by Princess Margaret and lastly Prince Philip. As Prince Philip's foot went down on to the stair immediately in front of me, his foot caught the end of Princess

13

BOB HOPE

with

MOIRA LISTER

JERRY DESMONDE

and

THE HOPE REPERTORY COMPANY

14 **FINALE** by THE FULL COMPANY

God Save The Queen

Bob Hope in the programme for the 1954 Royal Variety Performance

71

Margaret's train and there was a loud sound of ripping fabric. He turned towards me and gave me a huge wink, which needless to say made my evening, particularly as he was one of the most handsome men I had ever seen. Nearly thirty years later, my daughter Linda, age seventeen, was equally smitten by his charm when he presented a gold Duke of Edinburgh's award to her on a snowy January day at Buckingham Palace.

11

The Day War Was Declared

One would suppose that the last place you would expect to be when war was announced would be in church. Mother and I went to St John's Church, Hove fairly regularly and on that particular Sunday — 3 September 1939 — we were there when the verger approached the Reverend McNutt, who was in the pulpit, and he stopped half-way through delivering his sermon. He then said to his patient congregation that he had an important announcement — something along the lines of, 'Sadly I have to tell you that our government's negotiations with Herr Hitler in Germany have failed to achieve a peaceful settlement and thus it has been announced by Mr Chamberlain, our Prime Minister, that this country is now at war with Germany.' There was a long pause and then he continued, 'If anybody here feels it right to leave the church at this moment in order to go home and be with members of their family, please feel free to do so.'

Hushed and horrified quiet conversation followed and most people began slowly to leave. Ma and I left and waited for the bus to take us along Church Road and back to Brighton. Not being one to keep my thoughts to myself and seething with the indignation of a sixteen-year-old who didn't fully understand, I asked Mother in the half-full bus of passengers, 'Why has God let us down? We have been praying for peace for weeks — now what will happen?' My poor embarrassed mother wept and I was told to be quiet. At this point an air-raid siren began to sound — a strange howling noise. The bus stopped and passengers got off and began running to get home. Mother said we should walk quickly as we were nearly home. We were soon entering the back of the Grand Hotel via the garages. Going into that large, strong and solid old building gave a sense of security.

Mother's first thought was to find my twelve-year-old brother Peter, who was nowhere to be seen. A page boy told her that Peter had gone fishing! So my father — already in the midst of trying to pacify a number of guests who wanted to pay their bills and leave for their various homes immediately — was dispatched to the end of the West Pier. Here he found Peter and several other fishermen who were blissfully unaware of events, and collected him to return him to his mother. At the end of the war, rather appropriately, Peter joined the Navy and became Able Seaman Smith.

At this time there is no doubt people were frightened and many feared the Germans would arrive all along the south coast, landing on the piers at all the seaside resorts from Kent to Hampshire. That same week, local Territorial Army units of sappers were to blow up the centre part of the length of all the piers to make landing more difficult. A tailpiece to this is that Frank Wilson, who was a sapper in the Royal Engineers, and who became my husband some years later, appropriately blew up the centre parts of the West Pier and the Palace Pier as well as the piers in Worthing, Bognor Regis, Eastbourne and Hastings!

Meanwhile my brother was being reprimanded for being so far away when 'danger was imminent'. I was sent to the ballroom, where trestle tables were laid out with hundreds of flat-pack cardboard boxes. These had to be assembled to carry our individual gas masks which we were ordered by the government to wear at all times on a length of string around our necks.

Later the same day I was asked by Mrs Marlow to go with her to the flat in Regency Square (which she and Mr M had rented because the hotel was so full) in order to help her pack, as they were anxious to return home to London. As we walked together in the sunshine along the almost deserted seafront there was a strange eerie silence — a foreboding of the disastrous times to come. For a short while a sense of national apprehension prevailed, but this soon went in spite of the air-raid shelters being built and access to the beaches prohibited by the placing of barbed-wire obstructions all along the coast. Indeed, life returned to almost normal. This early period became known as 'the phoney war'. Strangely enough, there was no suggestion that we could be in any danger living on the seventh floor of such a prominent building on the seafront which, had the Germans attacked the south coast, would have been an easy target from the sea.

The most obvious effects of the early months of the war on Peter and me were that he could no longer go fishing off the end of the West Pier and *Rusalka*, our canoe, was out of reach on the other side of the barbed wire on the beach. Before long, however, Peter went back to his boarding school in Sevenoaks and I went back to Brighton Art School.

During the 'phoney war', before the very real war began, even more unusual and interesting people continued to visit the hotel (and probably more so because it was no longer so easy to go abroad for holidays). About this time I became friendly with the three Mawby sisters — triplets who came regularly to dances and Sunday lunches with their parents. I also went to have tea with them several times and we became quite friendly. They were all strikingly attractive blondes — about my age, and always wore exactly the same outfits in three different pastel shades. I was reminded of them and their outfits some years later when I went to a garden party at Buckingham Palace — amazingly, the Queen, her sister Princess Margaret and the Queen Mother each wore very similar dresses in pale blue, yellow and pink.

The Mawbys were nice girls but very shy. Their mother was a pushy woman who not only kept a very strict eye on them, but also let it be known that they had all recently returned from Hollywood, where they had been in several films — and consequently they became know as 'the Starlets'! They would always be sitting with their parents looking rather bored!

75

At the time they were living in one of the six or so large houses at the far west end of Hove near the lagoon. Each house had its own private beach and the girls' rooms had balconies overlooking the shingle — lovely in the summer. However, they found them a bit scary in the winter when there were south-westerly gales blowing into their rooms, especially when the heavy seas caused pebbles to be thrown up high enough to crash against the glass. One of these houses now belongs to former Beatle, Paul McCartney.

When we moved away from Brighton during the war, I lost contact with the Mawby sisters, but strangely enough had tragic news of them many years later. Soon after my marriage to Frank Wilson, I was reading some letters written to him by his father when Frank was in France with the Royal Engineers. One of the pieces of local news he wrote was that the head foreman of F.T. Wilson and Sons (the family builders) had been called to help clear up following an air raid at Marine Gate Flats in Black Rock — now just above Brighton Marina. Jack Walters, the foreman, had to help the emergency services to remove the body of a young woman who had been blown by the bomb blast down a lift shaft and killed. It was one of the triplets, who had been standing near the lift door with her mother and her two sisters, waiting for the lift to come, and the bomb blast sent her crashing down the lift shaft while leaving the others behind unharmed. A dreadful thing to happen.

A year or so before the war, there was talk by my parents of sending me to a finishing school in Liège in Belgium. Pa had become friendly with the then manager of the Arsenal football team who had a daughter the same age and the idea was that we should go together. I remember seeing the school prospectus and thinking that it looked a bit bleak and I wanted to stay at the Art School. Fate stepped in and when war was declared, the idea was abandoned.

For several years before the war, the Davis Cup tennis team came to stay for a week's holiday prior to their major tennis tournament and Pa arranged for them to have the courts available for practice at the Hotel Metropole, next door to the Grand. They were pleasant,

76

well-behaved young men, but the nearest I ever got to knowing them was in the lift — with 'Old Tom' keeping an eye on me!

Another group who came frequently during the early months of the Second World War were pilots from BOAC — British Overseas Airways Corporation. At the time they were flying over to France with mail for the Forces, but when the weather was too bad for flying from Croydon airport, they came and stayed in the hotel — all expenses paid! I became friendly with several of the younger men and there was one in particular, John, who was a good dancer. It became obvious that Pa did not approve of him — for reasons I never knew. On one Saturday evening when I was dancing with him a page boy came over to us and said, 'Miss Pam, I have a message from your father. He says you may dance with this gentleman, but you may not leave the ballroom!' Most embarrassing, especially for the young page boy!

One very strange happening during the early months of the war was its 'postponement' due to the extreme weather during the winter of 1939-1940. Referred to as the 'Great Frost', one of the severest frosts on record started just before Christmas when even the sea froze off Felpham near Bognor Regis. Heavy rain fell in January and it was so cold everything it touched became encased in ice — apparently some poor birds were frozen by their feet to branches of trees and roofs of houses. I remember hearing that the Mayor of Brighton and others on a long cold train journey from London to Brighton lasting seven hours were kept entertained by members of the 'Crazy Gang', including Bud Flanagan and Chesney Allen. The strange thing was that all references to the weather were censored for a couple of weeks for fear the information might be used by the enemy — but it turned out that the rest of Europe was just as bad!

It was during the spring of 1940 that I had a romantic encounter which not only caused fireworks at the time but also had impact much later in my life. I am pretty sure it was probably Easter Sunday — a beautiful sunny day and the so called phoney war was about to end.

I was sitting with Ma on the hotel terrace near the main front door having tea when a very handsome young army officer in uniform came over and asked if he could take me out for a spin in his new car — an open-topped sports coupé — and also give Ma's black Aberdeen Scottie dog a walk on the downs. The young man's name was Kenneth Newton, and he and his mother were visiting his elderly grandparents, Sir James and Lady Garner, who lived in the hotel. Our families knew each other well — his grandparents had lived mainly in London before the war where Sir James had a big tannery in Bermondsey, but were regular visitors to the Grand throughout my childhood. They were both immensely proud of their only grandson, who they told us had become the youngest major in the British Army.

Kenneth came quite often to visit his grandparents, who, although they had a flat in Knightsbridge, came to stay in the hotel every Easter and Christmas — always having the same rooms, so the hotel was a second home to them. We knew each other in rather a vague sort of way — I suppose the five-year difference in our ages was a lot when we were children, but we did play a lot of table tennis together. Many years later I did come to know Kenneth rather well — we were married in 1980, but sadly separated in 1988.

On that well-remembered sunny Sunday I would have been seventeen and Kenneth twenty-two. Off we went to Rottingdean, he no doubt driving fast along the wide cliff-top road, showing off his skills with his 'new toy' (he was still doing this 40 years later). We parked the car behind the village, near the edge of the downs, and walked with the dog for a while. Eventually Kenneth suggested we sat down on the grass for a rest. I agreed willingly, still young and innocent enough not to be in the least bit worried that anything untoward might happen! Within a very few minutes he was sound asleep, snoring. There I sat — near, but not too near — somewhat embarrassed by this large, inert, but still attractive young male in uniform, who continued to sleep for what must have been an hour or more.

When he eventually woke he became embarrassingly apologetic, saying he had been out on manoeuvres all the previous night —

probably true. Standing up, straightening his immaculate uniform, he then suggested he took me out to dinner, saying it was the least he could do to make up for his inability to stay awake and entertain me. Driving back through Rottingdean, we found a restaurant right on the edge of the cliffs overlooking the sea. We must have enjoyed each other's company because it was about 10 p.m. when we arrived back in the garage at the rear of the Grand.

Then ... oh dear! Both families must have been on the terrace watching for our return because as we drove into the garage, there they all were, standing in a line at the top of the steps in front of the double doors. There was the most dreadful scene; my mother weeping — almost hysterical — and my father, absolutely furious (probably more concerned about losing such wealthy, regular clients). My mother was implying I could have lost my virginity and/or we could both have been killed in a car accident. Kenneth's mother Gladys didn't say much, probably furious that her perfect son could be accused, if only indirectly, of ungentlemanly behaviour on both counts. I think Lady G was very embarrassed but sympathetic towards us — my mother had worked herself up into an unreasonable frenzy and I suspect Grandfather James was slightly amused and bored by it all. Eventually I was sent to my bedroom on the seventh floor, well out of harm's way, and Kenneth rejoined his regiment late that evening and we didn't meet again for 10 or more years until quite by accident we (with our respective spouses) bumped into each other at Narbonne station in south-west France.

In early May 1940 life took a very different turn. On returning from art school one afternoon I was sent by my father down to the kitchens to help make sandwiches. Large tables had been cleared and the few remaining staff and guests were all busy — I have no recollection of anyone telling me why or for whom we made the sandwiches! The following morning I dressed and went to go down to the dining room for breakfast as usual. On reaching the top of the main staircase I was greeted with the quite extraordinary sight of hundreds of khaki-clad soldiers with their boots on, strewn on every tread of the seven flights of stairs. They were all sound asleep, in various postures of total exhaustion, most of them with their rifles next to them and some had bandages round their heads. Not one took the slightest notice of me as I stepped over and between them, eventually reaching the old staff spiral staircase — a shortcut I knew well. Then it was breakfast as usual, while several waiters — my friends — tried to explain what little they knew: 'This was our army escaping from France.' Within days we all knew about Dunkirk — the real war had begun. After breakfast I left to go to art school, cycling along the seafront as usual.

Following Dunkirk, the Grand was requisitioned by the army, who occupied the hotel for the duration of the war and everybody had to leave. By this time many staff and all guests had gone, except for two elderly sisters, Mrs Hodgson and Mrs Isaacson, who had lived there as permanent residents for the previous 38 years. Permanent residents who could afford to make the Grand their home and enjoy all the luxury and comforts provided an important source of regular revenue for the hotel. Some of this group of guests became real friends of my parents and were always very kind to Peter and myself, sometimes giving us special presents. One kind lady, Mrs Bond, brought back a toy koala bear for me from her trip to Australia — one of the last real koala bears to be stuffed for export, which, since I gave it to my granddaughter, has become rather bald!

Mrs Hodgson and Mrs Isaacson always dressed all in black with high white lace collars and looked like Queen Victoria and Queen Mary. Indeed, they behaved as if royalty. Each had a silver-topped black Malacca walking cane. Mrs Hodgson would wave hers at staff when she wanted to make a point. Peter and I avoided them. My father, however, was extremely patient and tactful with them — particularly with Mrs Hodgson. They were very wealthy women and ideal permanent residents, tipping all the staff well.

When the hotel was requisitioned by the Army, Mrs Hodgson flatly refused to leave and poor Mrs Isaacson, the younger sister, wept copiously when told that they had to go. Eventually Mrs Hodgson was carried down the stairs (from their second-floor suite) in a special chair, followed by her weeping sister. They were treated like royalty by the staff, who lined the main hall to the front door, some of the maids curtsying and the porters and pages cheering and clapping. Mrs Hodgson died soon after — the shock had been too much — but Mrs Isaacson lived on alone in a nursing home for a few years — a sad end to a pair of remarkable women. After the war, the table where they sat in the dining room by a marble pillar was always referred to by Mr Pozzi, the head waiter, as 'the two ghosts' table'.

50 YEARS AGO

BRIGHTON'S two biggest hotels, the Grand and the Metropole, closed their doors today. The Grand, opened 80 years ago, was built on the site of the old Brighton battery, hence Cannon Place, Cannon Street and Artillery Street. Among the last to leave was an 88-year-old lady who had been resident at the hotel for 38 years. "It was the most poignant situation I have ever experienced," Mr Sydney Smith, manager of the Grand, told the Argus. (1940).

A moving moment for the Grand's eldest residents, Mrs Isaacson and Mrs Hodgson (The *Argus*, 1990)

12

London and the Blitz

With Peter at boarding school in Sevenoaks in Kent in 1940, Mother and I went with my father to London, where Pa became manager of the Hans Crescent Hotel (which belonged to the same parent company, Spiers and Ponds) behind Harrods in Knightsbridge.

When Peter broke up from school in July he joined us in London, and Mother would take us for fresh air into Hyde Park, where we watched huge air-raid shelters and gun sites being built and barrage balloons being erected. I absolutely hated London. It was hot and smelly and I missed the sea and all my friends. My way of coping with the misery was to read *Gone with the Wind* — a real tome of a book — in a week, ignoring anyone and everyone around me. Reading was my method of escape which I have used all my life.

After a couple of weeks or so, Pa managed to arrange for me to work in Harrods — very convenient, as it was on our doorstep! I worked there for ten shillings (50p) a week, which, somewhat to my father's disgust, I spent on silk stockings for 1s. 6d. — with a staff discount of ten per cent, I decided it made them a real bargain!

Harrods was fun — the other girls were always friendly and helpful to me; they arrived at 9 a.m. as the store opened and would gather in the store room behind the dress/separates department, to compare notes on the number of incendiary bombs they had put out the previous night — they all did 'fire-watching' duties most nights, which meant being with the ARP (Air Raid Precautions) wardens on

The Hans Crescent Hotel, Knightsbridge. Our flat was at the top right in this photograph

the tops of large buildings near their homes and dealing with these small, unpleasant but effective bombs, using stirrup pumps and sand.

I became part of what was called the 'Junior Contingent' and was placed in different departments every two weeks. My favourite was the book department — unfortunately the temptation to read some of the books was too great and eventually I would disappear into the loo to read. When this was discovered I was duly reprimanded. Sometimes I had to go down to the huge stores in the basement which existed under the whole area of the vast shop and beyond.

Because the distance between departments was so far, there were small motorised trucks to carry the goods, and staff were able get rides on them, which was fun.

The London Blitz started in early September 1940. That day Peter and I had gone to swim in the pool at Roehampton Sports Club — half an hour or so away by bus. We left the pool about six in the evening but could not find a bus for our return journey, as there was very little traffic about and not many people. We began to walk and eventually a bus came along and stopped and we got on. There were few passengers and the conductor told us that his bus would not be going all the way to Knightsbridge because air raids had begun — he pointed towards east London where we could see smoke filling the sky above buildings. As we got closer the smoke became red and orange, coloured by the fires below. Somewhere in Kensington we had to get off and were told the driver was returning to the depot to put the bus in the garage and go home to his family. We then walked the rest of the way — by then I think we were becoming accustomed to strange things happening and I don't remember being unduly worried.

Ma was very relieved to see us. I had a quick meal because I was going to the theatre with a friend, Desmond Hone, a dentist, who was on leave from the Navy. My friendship with Desmond was another connection to living in the Grand. His mother lived there for a whole year when she was the Mayoress of Brighton, to support her father who was the Mayor.

Desmond arrived and we found a taxi to the London Palladium. There we saw a musical comedy-type show with the 'Crazy Gang' — my favourites were Flanagan and Allen, who sang, danced and made jokes. It was very warm in the theatre and I recall being annoyed with Desmond for removing his jacket — not quite the thing to do!

The whole performance was very noisy and when we left the sky was bright red with the fires burning in London's East End; the noise of exploding bombs and gunfire was intense. We hadn't noticed it at all inside the theatre because the show was so loud! Again, with no taxis or buses in sight, we began to walk down Oxford Street towards Piccadilly Circus. Several times as the noise seemed to get

THE CRAZY GANG

BUD FLANAGAN

NERVO & KNOX

NAUGHTON & GOLD

| JIMMY | TEDDY | BUD | CHARLIE | JIMMY |
| NERVO | KNOX | FLANAGAN | NAUGHTON | GOLD |

The Crazy Gang put on a great show during the war

closer we dived into various basements being used as shelters, and we asked if any of the bus or taxi drivers who had taken shelter in them would drive us to Knightsbridge. All refused — some British were not very brave that evening — so Desmond decided we would continue to walk. When we reached Piccadilly we went into the Athenaeum Club, where I knew an old friend from the Grand, Nessie Kain, was working as a receptionist. She gave us coffee and we managed to telephone our parents, then we continued on our way, walking back to Hans Crescent. Desmond knew he was responsible for getting me home and that my parents would have been very cross if he hadn't done so, and that was all we could think about. We had no idea of the imminent devastation.

In spite of the then continuous air raids, people in London did their best to get on with their lives as usual. On another occasion Desmond and I went to an evening concert in the Albert Hall — not too far away from Hans Crescent. Being able to get to places on the tube trains became important because during the raids most of the buses stopped running and it was much safer to be below ground. After the concert we walked to the nearby tube station, paid for our tickets — it was only one stop back to Knightsbridge — but when we got down to the platform it was crowded with people who had gone down to spend the night there in safety. All the platforms were packed to overflowing with families and their children, some in deckchairs, others sitting on the cold stone floor wrapped in blankets, some already sleeping. It was only with difficulty that we managed to step between them to get into the train — itself already very full. But we managed and got home quite quickly. By September the evenings were drawing in and the raids started earlier, so most people didn't go out after dark unless they had to.

The next month, still at the age of seventeen, I went to Adastra House in the Kingsway near the Strand with Nessie who was enlisting in the WAAF (Women's Auxiliary Air Force). On the spur of the moment I also decided to join. A long interview followed, with a very smart WAAF officer who asked endless questions about my education and background. During the interview I succeeded in giving my date of birth as January 1922, making me just over eighteen. When we had finished I got up to leave, but the WAAF officer called me back to confirm my date of birth. Taken by surprise I hesitated, and had to confess I had given the wrong date. She laughed and said, 'Come back next year.' I was too young!

The Hans Crescent was an old well-built hotel with very thick walls and considered reasonably safe unless it had a direct hit by a bomb. To begin with, we had bedrooms up on the fourth floor but after a few weeks the bombing got more intense and it was decided that we would move down to bedrooms on the first floor. Pa subsequently had beds put all along the sidewalls in the wide corridor, head to foot! So when things got even worse we could sleep out there, away from the glass of the windows and the very large winter garden (conservatory) at the rear of the building.

In the room opposite mine there was an elderly lady — a Russian princess — tall and dressed all in black, day and night. Each time she came out of her room to sleep in the corridor, she brought several cages of canary birds with her. They smelled somewhat and the poor frightened birds made a horrid squeaky noise all night. Whilst Ma objected to sleeping in the corridor I was young enough to sleep through regardless — until the night we were hit!

That night, in November 1940, when the noise began it was worse than usual. Apparently large naval guns were firing on the bombers, from sites in Hyde Park. Thus I decided to go to bed in the corridor. Ma said she would sleep in her bedroom, but would come out and join me if the noise got worse. I don't think Pa even got to bed during those weeks. I was woken by the whooshing sound of bombs coming down — by then we knew about 'baskets' of bombs, usually six bombs at a time. Following the second 'whoosh' — which was nearer — I shouted to Ma, who shouted back to me saying, 'Don't worry I am next to you, put your head under the pillow.' Of course everything was very dark and we could not see each other, but she had come out on the landing and was in the next bed. The next two bombs had hit the winter garden at the back of the hotel — the first two had hit Harrods and the last two made holes in the road — big enough to put a bus in!

We staggered up from our beds (by then we always went to bed fully dressed), surprised to find we were still alive. The air was so thick with dust it was hard to breathe. I have hated fireworks ever since — particularly the smell of cordite, something I believe is in both bombs and fireworks. I don't recall a lot of fuss; the ARP wardens and police were there almost immediately.

The person who was the most upset was the Russian princess because all the canaries were silent — I suppose they had been killed by the fumes and the shock. We were escorted down to the front entrance hall and the first thing I did was to disappear into the hall porter's lobby and remove the curling rags from my hair — there were no rollers in those days — as I didn't want to be seen in them. There seemed to be a lot of people milling about and eventually we were all escorted by the ARP to spend the rest of the night in the air-raid shelter because the hotel was considered structurally unsafe.

With all the guests in a group, we turned out of Hans Crescent into Sloane Street towards the shelter. As we passed the large car showrooms on the corner, a very large plate glass window (which had been covered with wide sticky tape) fell out on to the pavement, just missing us. Nobody batted an eyelid — after our earlier experiences of that night this was a very minor event!

The shelter was two levels below the street — large with temporary wooden shelves serving as bunk beds, one above the other. My poor mother was desperately worried about Father who had gone to help the ARP men in Lowndes Square where gas mains had exploded, causing massive casualties. Much to our relief he appeared at daylight, okay, but very tired and dirty.

We returned to the Hans Crescent Hotel and by the end of the day all the guests had left to stay in other hotels. A few staff remained to help clear up. I was shown a bedroom on the third floor where an elderly man had been staying; the huge chimney from the roof above had collapsed, dropping right through the floor above, before landing on his bed. He had apparently been sitting in an armchair all night and was relatively unharmed when they finally found him the next morning.

The hotel dining room had a large old oak circular table which was used for buffets. For the following week we slept in the basement bar and ate at the table — just Ma, Pa and me — and every time the air-raid sirens went off we had to dive underneath! My bedroom, which overlooked the winter garden, was badly damaged. The lead frames of the windows had crumpled up into large ball-like shapes, one of which went straight through my pillow — but a large vase of pink carnations was still in place and intact on the dressing table; blast shock waves do extraordinary things!

Pa decided he had to remain in the hotel to try and salvage what remained — furniture, tableware, linen and so on — but said that Ma and I should leave London as the Blitz was getting worse every night. Ma refused to leave Pa, so I was sent to stay with my old school friend, Margie Miller, in Hove. Ma and Pa came with me in a taxi to Surbiton Station, because both Victoria and Waterloo had been bombed. The usual ride of fifteen minutes took two hours plus, because the streets were obstructed by fire engines and hosepipes and all the palaver of clearing up and rescuing people after the previous night's air raid. It was almost dark when we reached Surbiton and Pa put me into an empty carriage then hurried back to my mother waiting in the taxi. If she had not been left in the cab, it almost certainly would have been taken by another fare — taxis were like gold dust — and then they would have been utterly stranded in Surbiton!

Minutes later I was joined by a girl in uniform, who turned out to be a Canadian nurse. We never saw each other's faces because by then it was dark with only a very few blue-painted lights on the train. Suddenly the whole train filled with soldiers, who packed in like sardines, sitting on the floor of the compartments and the corridors and even on each other's knees. At this point, we two lone females realised we were even more scared of so many unknown and unseen men than we were of the bombs!

We managed to talk and get to know each other a little amongst the noisy, chaotic conditions of the carriage and finally the train departed. It took between seven and eight hours to reach Brighton (normally a one-hour train ride), crawling along in pitch darkness. The driver must have been trying to see if the track in front had been damaged — we could see fires and hear guns and bombs to the east side of the train not many miles away. My new friend and I held hands for comfort throughout the journey. When we reached Brighton around midnight we parted, never to meet again.

I managed to reach Hove and was met by Mrs Miller, Margie's kindly mum, and several weeks of peace and fun followed with my old school chum and her younger sister Isabel. My main concerns were for my parents still in London and also that shrapnel might come through the roof of the little flat over the garages where we three girls were living.

Even though we were seventeen, Margaret's father did not like us to go out after dark. This made for long evenings, but at that time we both knew several nice young men and I recall a lot of jolly evenings, playing games and drinking coffee — all very cosy and away from the bombs.

13

Best Part of the War — Lynton and Lynmouth, North Devon

Following the bombing of and around the Hans Crescent, it was considered the hotel could no longer function. Just before Christmas 1940, Pa was appointed manager of the Valley of the Rocks Hotel in Lynton, North Devon. Imagine being away from the bombs and by the sea again! Complete bliss — a bedroom looking across Lynmouth to Exmoor and the sea; a double bed and an eiderdown with pink roses!

It was decided that it was too dangerous for Peter to remain at his boarding school in Kent, because Sevenoaks was located in what was known as 'Bomb Alley'. This was where the German aircraft had a nasty habit of jettisoning any bombs they had failed to drop on London, rather than fly back to Germany with live bombs on board. To my great relief it was decided that Peter would go to West Buckland school in Devon about 10 miles away (just south-west of Barnstable), where he would be safe.

I believe I travelled alone to Reading station, where I met up with Ma, Pa and Peter, and we travelled to Barnstable in Devon from where we were taken by taxi on to Lynton. Being all together again and away from the air raids was wonderful and it was almost Christmas! It really was heaven to be in lovely countryside and by the sea once more, the peace and quiet very special for us all.

The hotel was much smaller than the Grand or the Hans Crescent

With Ma in the garden of the Valley of the Rocks Hotel, Lynton, North Devon

and stood high up next to the Church at the top of the woods and the road leading down to Lynmouth. Almost all the guests had come from London to avoid the bombs. They were the lucky ones, able to afford to leave the dangers behind them, and most lived at the Valley of the Rocks for a year or more until it was safer to return to the capital.

It was an unusual building. The entrance was up several steps and through the front door, directly into the main lounge in the centre. The corridors to the bedrooms were on three floors and were contained by tiers of wrought-iron balustrades surrounding and overlooking the large open space above the lounge. All the other public rooms led off the main lounge and the dining-room windows faced the Bristol Channel to the north. At night we could see great fires burning in the distance in Wales, where Swansea was frequently being bombed.

Ma and Pa lived in the manager's apartment on the ground floor overlooking the churchyard. My bedroom was up on the second floor looking out over Lynmouth to Countisbury Hill, the wide open spaces of Exmoor and across the sea to South Wales. I had a small double bed with a pretty silk eiderdown decorated with large pink roses on a black background. Peter would often cycle home from his school, usually with his friend Frank Slann whose parents owned the large café very near to the hotel which sold Devon clotted cream teas. The horrors of the Blitz were soon forgotten.

I spent many happy hours gazing out of the window at the wonderful view, and at night there was often a long line of small twinkling lights going slowly up Countisbury Hill — army vehicles going out on to the moors on night manoeuvres. The Royal Engineers were stationed all around and had their Officers' Mess in Lynmouth, where they frequently hosted parties, to which I and other local girls were invited. There was always dancing and singing and several of the young men were good pianists. One of them, Jimmy, was given permission by the local rector to play the organ in Lynton Church and when I went with him to listen, he tried very hard to teach me to play — not very successfully.

Beth Lord, one of the girls I accompanied to the Mess, became a lifelong friend. She worked hard in the Bath Hotel in Lynmouth which belonged to her mother — her father had died just before the war began. Beth eventually married one of the sappers at Brompton Oratory after the war and I was her bridesmaid.

During my time in Devon I met a young Scottish officer with whom I fell seriously in love — I was 18 and he was 23. The whole romance lasted only a few weeks and all I recall was feeling that life had become a beautiful dream. To this day I can remember the sensation of living in a kind of wonderful bubble or on a heavenly cloud, quite separate from everyone and everyday life. Mostly we just danced together in the Officers' Mess, drove in his jeep on nearby Exmoor and walked along the cliff path, known as the North Walk, and back through the Valley of the Rocks. We both knew that one day soon he would be posted away and that both our immediate futures were unknown due to the war.

That moment came very suddenly and that was that. All I ever heard was a brief letter from him ending, 'Yours forever, Iain.' Mother was the only person who sensed how deeply this had affected me and she became very concerned when I lost weight — I was already tall and thin so I couldn't have afforded to lose much more.

In spite of this abortive love affair, my time in Lynton and Lynmouth, though barely lasting a year, remains one of my happiest memories. Brother Peter and I went riding whenever we could save enough money. Riding over Exmoor on the sure-footed Exmoor ponies was glorious, whatever the weather. Gradually I managed to acquire a proper riding outfit: jodhpurs bought for me in Minehead by Ma and Pa for my birthday, and soon after a much-needed riding mac with proper straps inside to go round my legs and stop it flapping. A proper crop with a bone handle was an Easter present and finally a lovely tweed hacking jacket was given to me by Coral Browne, the actress, in return for walking her dog. Coral was one of several interesting people who were living in the Valley of the Rocks Hotel to escape from the London air raids. She later became very famous for a film she made about her meetings with Guy Burgess, the spy who was living as an exile in Moscow. Sometimes as a special treat I would go with some hotel guests to the Lynton cinema, a very small converted church hall, and Coral would knit furiously all through the films.

Briefly, but very memorably, I had an amazing musical experience. I was walking Ma's Scottie dog and had gone down from Lynton to Lynmouth via the funicular railway and was going past the little concert hall. All the doors and windows were wide open as it was a beautiful, sunny summer's day, when I heard this fantastic voice. It was Joan Hammond, the famous Australian soprano. She had been stranded in London when the war proper started and, like many others who could afford to do so, had come away to escape the Blitz. With her on the stage were two other women — her accompanist and her secretary. Eventually she spotted me listening at the door-way and beckoned me in — dog and all — and asked me to sit down and listen. It was a wonderful experience. For the first time I began to appreciate how very beautiful a fine and powerful voice could be.

I was fortunate enough to meet her again later, when I was on leave staying with Beth at the Bath Hotel in Lynmouth and a group of us went to a very old pub in the middle of Exmoor called the Ring O' Bells. And once again, several years later, Ma and I went to a concert when she was singing in the Dome Theatre in Brighton. As we were leaving, Ma, who understood how thrilled I was to hear that superb voice again, said 'You must go and speak to her.' We waited outside the stage door for her to leave, and as she appeared, Ma gave me a gentle push, saying, 'Have a quick word.' To my amazement, she remembered me and said how much she would have liked to meet for a drink, but as she was returning to Australia in two days, sadly it was not to be.

The authoress Radclyffe Hall visited the Valley of the Rocks fre-quently with her friend Lady Una Troubridge. Peter and I went with them for rides over Exmoor and Radclyffe Hall was very friendly towards me, paying me compliments, and saying I had a 'very good seat' on my horse — the significance of which I will explain. She always dressed in men's suits, collar and tie and in the evening wore a dinner jacket, trousers and a black tie. Her companion wore long evening gowns and expensive furs. They would go straight into the bar, where Pa greeted them with their first drink on the house. Later, they would come out to sit in the lounge for coffee; needless to say, they attracted a good deal of curiosity.

My mother told me that Radclyffe Hall had written a book which had been banned from shops and libraries. Mother was somewhat Victorian in her attitudes and refused to tell me any more. She was adamant there were to be no more questions. I don't believe she was ever aware that Peter and I knew this strange pair of women quite well through our rides together.

The reason Ma took this attitude became clear some years later when, quite by chance, I found the book *The Well of Loneliness* by Radclyffe Hall on the shelf of the Hove public library. At some point in the mid-1950s not only had it been reinstated, but it had become considered a classic. I have read it a couple of times since. Whilst written as a novel, it is mainly about her and the many miserable years she spent both before and after realising she was a lesbian. She found a degree of happiness in her partnership with Una Troubridge, but it was an uneasy relationship — Lady Troubridge had a great deal of money from previous husbands, while Radclyffe Hall, who was known as 'John', had to struggle with her writing to maintain her financial independence.

The war hardly seemed to affect Lynton and Lynmouth, there was plenty to be enjoyed! Pa did a lot of walking, which he always liked, and sometimes I went with him. The longest walk we did was to the Hunters Inn at Heddon's Mount, several miles to the west of Lynton, up and down some very steep hills, through very lovely Devon lanes — nearly fourteen miles. My legs ached for days after! Riding was much more enjoyable, letting the horses do all the work! Although the horses came from the riding stables we rode frequently enough to have our favourites, and mine was a lovely Exmoor pony called Tuppence. In the autumn when the hedges were profuse with the largest blackberries I have ever seen, I would bend forward over his neck to pick some, but Tuppence always ate the best and biggest before I could reach them!

At a friend's house we made lots of blackberry jelly and in spite of the sugar rationing we produced enough to sell at the church fete. I have never forgotten the smell of the jelly cooking — the rich red Devon soil must have contributed something special.

Peter would go stag hunting, which was very popular with the locals, but having seen a stag jump off a cliff edge to escape the hounds, I would never join them.

My favourite walk was along Watersmeet, down in Lynmouth,

Preparing to take Tuppence for a ride on Exmoor

where the East Lyn and West Lyn rivers met, the sparkling waters rushing down from the moors over the rocks with a canopy of trees above. During the war years petrol was severely rationed and we did not have a car, so by walking and riding I got to know this very special part of north Devon very well.

There was a bus service which went into Minehead and this was quite an adventure. When the large, old, single-decker bus returned from Minehead and began to ascend Porlock Hill, it shuddered to a halt and all the passengers got out and pushed and eventually it reached the top! For the younger ones this was all part of wartime fun — but not so good for the older passengers!

14

Early WAAF Years of 2066191, Corporal Sydney-Smith

By the summer of 1941, I had become restless, feeling I needed to become involved in the war effort. I applied to join the WRNS (Women's Royal Naval Service) partly because I liked their uniform, but also because I thought I might at least be stationed near the sea! They wrote back and told me there was a six-month waiting list, so I then applied to the WAAF. On 2 September 1941 I went to the recruitment offices in Exeter, where, following a routine medical examination and an interview, I was accepted and told to go home and wait to be called up. On 30 October 1941 I went by train to a very large air force camp at Innsworth in Gloucestershire and was enrolled. I was eighteen and a half years old.

On the day I departed to report for service with the WAAF, Pa put me on the bus to Minehead to catch the train to Bristol. We walked from the hotel, Pa carrying my small suitcase, to the funicular railway to take us down to Lynmouth and then walked to the small bus station. I think and hope I remember a peck on my cheek when Pa said, 'This new life will teach you a thing or two my girl — it's what you need,' and I got on the bus and he walked away. I think my parents saw life in the services as a kind of very strict finishing school. Perhaps it was, but in many ways it was a great adventure which I could not have enjoyed more! It was like nothing I had ever experienced before, and even the few weeks in the large reception centre had their moments.

On our third day at RAF Innsworth Reception Centre in Gloucestershire, various RAF officers interviewed all the new arrivals individually, so that they could find out what kind of work we were suitable for. A very smart and attractive WAAF officer began by asking routine questions and filling in various forms. Needless to say I endeavoured to answer honestly, and fortunately this proved a good move because it became obvious that having always lived in hotels, I had no domestic ability at all and the only talent I had was art work and drawing, so she suggested I was assigned to be a 'Clerk Special Duties', which meant I was eventually posted to Fighter Command and served at 11 Group Headquarters at Uxbridge. But I almost botched it all up when I was asked why I was not applying for a commission, as I had attended a Girls' Public Day School Trust school. I replied that I didn't think I was ready to hold a commission until I knew more about the Air Force. She tried to convince me that I would enjoy being an officer, but to her obvious irritation I still refused and she struck a large red line across my papers. I never really regretted the refusal until three to four years later when, tired with endless night duty and hungry, I came to realise the WAAF officers were better housed and better fed!

I never did attain great heights of promotion — in spite of doing several jobs of some worth — because at vital moments my unfortunate habit of (usually) 'knowing better' and my socialist inclinations wrecked my chances. After almost five years I was still a corporal! By that time, however, I had had a fascinating career, with spells in both Fighter Command and Bomber Command.

It was a very cold and very wet November, and we were sleeping and living in large Nissen huts — about sixty women in a hut. During the first night we were unable to sleep for the cold, and then I remembered the old lady on the park bench from my childhood, wrapped in newspapers that kept her warm at night.

The next day I managed to acquire several newspapers from the NAAFI (Navy, Army and Air Force Institute). We had iron beds topped by three 'biscuits' which formed a mattress in sections so they could be stacked up separately for inspection. I spread the newspapers under the biscuits to stop the draughts which came up between them and also between the army blankets. That night I was as warm as toast and the following day all sixty young women followed my example. At night the sound of rustling newspaper was weird — nevertheless, I became suddenly very popular and had endless offers from my fellow rookies (new recruits) to set my hair and paint my nails. They also offered to polish my shoes and buttons for me — which was just as well because due to my previous cosseted life in five-star hotels, I hadn't a clue! At home all I did was to place my shoes outside my bedroom door for the porters to collect, clean and return! When it came to cleaning out the tall black chimney-like coal fire in the hut, that was a different matter and I had to write and ask my father how to do this and how to light the fire. Discovering that the NAAFI sold 'fire lighters' was a boon.

In general terms, on reflection, I think that we were very well cared for by the welfare side of the RAF (except for the mice, the difficulties of keeping warm, tedious food, and long, erratic working hours). During the first weeks at Innsworth Reception Centre we were shown excellent and explicit American films on hygiene. I well remember those concerning childbirth, details of how a baby 'was made', how it grew inside and details of the results of unprotected and indiscriminate sex. As my mother, like many of her generation, was quite unable to explain the facts of life, I was both relieved and pleased to be told how it all happened!

At that stage of the war large numbers of women in their early twenties who were not in reserved occupations were being conscripted. Many of them came from very poor homes and the WAAF medical orderlies had in some cases to insist on bathing them in disinfectant. These girls were usually employed as WAAF cooks and butchers. Also everybody was given an 'FFI' (Free From Infection), which involved intense inspection of head and scalp for nits!

The next landmark in my new life was the pink cotton bra which was issued to us all, along with the rest of our uniform. This was the first time that I had had a bra — Ma thought they were unladylike and as I did not have much to put in one, I was not bothered. But my new pink and rather stiff cotton bra was a joy — I was really grown-up now and nearly nineteen!

From bras we move up to Morecambe Bay, near Blackpool in Lancashire — where the RAF did its best to turn raggle-taggle young women into smart service personnel. We were marched up and down the seafront in autumn gales until most of us were suffering agonies with our feet due to the new black lace-up shoes we were wearing — resulting in most of the women being confined to their quarters for a week by the medical officer, which was a much-needed rest.

The kindness of strangers was impressed on me early one winter's evening when I managed to get lost in Morecambe, by myself, and I asked an elderly lady for direction. She waited to see me onto the correct bus, then decided to not only come with me to ensure I got off at the right stop, but also insisted on paying my fare.

15

11 Group, Fighter Command and 'Y' Service

From Morecambe Bay in late 1941, I was posted to 11 Group Headquarters at Uxbridge, part of Fighter Command. The Operations Room ('Ops Room') was some two hundred feet below ground and heavily guarded by the RAF regiment. The whole vast underground complex held various offices and highly secret technical equipment. The main Ops Room was filled by a huge table on which was a map of southern England — from London round to Southampton — the area known as 11 Group and all divided by a grid system. On one side were two dais-like galleries, where the duty controller sat, plus various other officers and WAAFs. On the wall opposite was the information about the state of readiness and availability of all the fighter aircraft in 11 Group. This was updated continuously by RAF sergeants who went up stepladders that glided across the boards. There were several fighter stations known as 'sector stations' within 11 Group's control, including Tangmere, Kenley, Biggin Hill, Hornchurch and others. Most fighters were Spitfires or Hurricanes, the pilots spending time in huts at dispersal points around airfields waiting for orders to take off. These orders came from the Controller at 11 Group HQ, given first to the Sector Controller, who passed it on directly to the men waiting beside their planes at the dispersal points.

About 10 WAAFs stood at positions on the four sides of the

In the Ops Room at 11 Group, Fighter Command Headquarters, Uxbridge. I am the girl at far right on the lower dais, and Ronnie Adams, film star, was the Controller (2nd from right on the top dais)

Operations table in the Ops Room. Each WAAF wore a headset and a 'tube speaker', and used a long metal pole with a magnetic end to push small metal markers around the table. These indicated the aircraft's identity — 'friendly' or 'hostile' — the height it was flying at, and the number of planes. This information was constantly being updated as the alterations were passed to the WAAF 'plotters' on the headsets.

To begin with I became a 'plotter', and within a few weeks I plotted the very heavy raids on Southampton. Soon after this, when it became known that I had some drawing ability, I became part of the 'Raid Recording' team. Sergeant Yeo, who was in charge of the Raid Recording Office, had a great sense of humour. He had acquired an old pike which he used to joke he would use to defend 'his WAAFS' from the Germans. In the main Ops Room, there were three groups of forty WAAFs, forming three watches. Each watch did four

WAAF colleagues plotting aircraft movements in the Ops Room (I am second from left on the lower dais. (Photograph courtesy of Getty Images)

hours on duty, and eight hours off, with a free day every eight days. The Raid Recording team consisted of four girls from each watch and during a watch we would work in pairs, one hour recording by hand all that was happening on the Ops table, and then we went up to the Raid Recording Office above ground for the next hour and put all this information on to large charts — then back down to the Ops Room for one more hour and back to the office for another. All that we had recorded (from the Ops table) was then put onto the charts and was taken to the senior air officers, who would study them in detail in order to plan how the RAF would react to the next day's raids.

During the time I was a raid recorder I sat on the first level dais below the Controller, and worked alongside Rex Harrison, the film star. He was a Captain in the Army who coordinated the activity on

105

the Ops table for his Commander. Always very friendly, he would give me a swig from his brandy flask, particularly when I looked miserable and frozen after a 'square-bashing' session (marching up and down) on the parade ground — a kind man! Coincidentally, I met up again with Rex Harrison after the war when I was selling programmes at a Royal Command Performance in London. He recognised me and insisted on putting a considerable amount of money into my collection tin and also introduced me to Cecil Mills of Bertram Mills' Circus, who did likewise.

In 1942 living conditions for many service personnel were pretty awful. Uxbridge was a large old army camp with Nissen huts and some brick-built houses and several parade grounds. When I was there the WAAF were billeted in very small, very old terraced houses — actually condemned married quarters with no heating except for the smallest fireplaces possible, about 10 x 5 inches — almost impossible to get a fire going! We had to dig out our own coal from a coal stack about a quarter of a mile away and carry it back to the house, and even if we managed to light the fire, the heat was minimal and of course we had no hot water. To add to these delights, mice ran across us when were in bed trying to keep warm under the rough grey army blankets — I don't know which part of living there I disliked most.

Needless to say, when we were occasionally offered the chance of a bath in an unoccupied officer's quarters house, this was special. One evening I and my friend Polly collected our gear and went to enjoy a hot soak in a house on the camp to which we had been directed. Imagine our delight to go into a warm bathroom, with large bath towels, a bath mat, bath salts and talcum powder — what a treat! The bath was huge, so we both got in and immersed ourselves in this hot steamy luxury. After a few moments there was a loud banging on the bathroom door and a male voice shouted, 'Whose in 'ere? What's yer doing? Get yerselves out at once!' Terrified, we wrapped our pink bodies in the large fluffy bath towels and tentatively opened the bathroom door a couple of inches. There stood a large and tall red faced Flight Sergeant, apoplectic with fury, who

106

told us that we were in the bathroom of the AOC (Air Officer Commanding) and that we should 'Get out bloody fast,' adding that Mrs AOC was downstairs and having tea. Quickly we dressed and he shooed us downstairs. I suppose Mrs AOC had heard him shouting and she appeared in order to find out what was going on. It turned out that, needless to say, we were in the wrong house — we should have been in the house next door (which was empty), but all quarters were identical so it was an easily made mistake in the dark. Luckily, Mrs AOC had a sense of humour and when we apologised, she was charming — even giving us tea and cakes, which rounded off our embarrassing mistake happily, and all was forgiven. On our return to our cold, mouse-infested hovel, we had a very good laugh and a story to tell — but we were much more careful in future.

The lack of privacy, living with 16 to 60 other women in Nissen huts, resulted in us all being extremely modest. We all always undressed or dressed ourselves under our heavy blue greatcoats or our dressing gowns. During the cold weather it did keep us a bit warmer, especially when the door was often opened by WAAFs going in and out. I remember snow blowing in when we were in Norfolk.

About a year later I was posted to Kenley, a fighter station near Coulsdon in Surrey. There I became a 'stand in' for the position of 'Ops B' officer. Kenley and nearby Biggin Hill had both been very heavily attacked by the German Luftwaffe (German Air Force) during the early part of 1941. Prior to the Blitz in London, the Nazis had realised that they needed to destroy the Royal Air Force before they could defeat us enough for them to be able to invade. These attacks were serious and had destroyed the Biggin Hill Operations Room, but all the damage inflicted was quickly put to rights and each airfield returned to normal.

When I arrived at Kenley, among the Spitfire pilots were several young men who were to become legends for their role in successfully defending London during the dreadful bombing attacks. Among them was 'Cat's Eyes Cunningham', who had an exceptional ability to see in the dark, thus enabling him to shoot down large numbers of bombers during the night-time air raids on London and south-east England.

In the Kenley Ops Room I sat near to the Controller, keeping him informed about the state of aircraft ready for action. By this time we were still keeping as many planes ready for immediate action as possible, but in general things had become much less busy. It was an interesting job but not as exciting as being at 11 Group HQ, where it was possible to see the whole picture of what was happening.

I returned to Uxbridge after six months to be told that all 'Ops B' commissions for WAAFs had been closed. Nevertheless, another very interesting job was to be mine. I and three other WAAFs — all old friends from the RRO days — were to become part of a new section to be formed called ' "Y" service'. We were to learn how to interpret information which would be passed to us on special telephone lines from three new stations on the Kent coast where women language experts would translate from German into English messages they were hearing on very high frequency radios. The four of us then went to one of these new units on the cliffs at Capel-le-Ferne near Folkstone to learn what this was all about. Briefly, the language experts were picking up on their headsets, the voices of the German controllers in northern France as they gave instructions in German to their air crews; they also heard the Luftwaffe replying.

After a couple of weeks we four clerks returned to Fighter Command at Uxbridge where we sat next to the duty Controller and wrote all the information down in longhand, passing on anything that we considered relevant to the action occurring on the Ops Room table to the Controller. If the German Controller gave instructions on a certain radio frequency to a pilot we knew which airfield he was speaking from, and when the pilot was given a course to fly on we could work out where he was going to. As these new methods advanced, more and more vital facts were discovered. This work was of course highly secret — which was impressed on us often — but although we understood our own part in the scheme of things, the technicalities were way beyond us. Sometimes the messages heard and passed to us were quite personal — several times German pilots were heard saying they were going to crash or bale out. One young German kept asking his Controller to send his love to his mother just before he crashed.

Adolf Galland, known in Germany as a fighter ace, had seen action in the Spanish civil war and became a well-known voice at the 'Y' stations. In 1945, when he was shot down and wounded by American Mustangs, some of the German-speaking operators became very upset. These particular women were mainly Austrian Polish or Jewish Germans who had escaped to England from Nazi Germany before the war began — needless to add, they were very strictly vetted before being employed on 'Y' service.

Whilst I was at Capel we spent our days observing how these women worked and returned to our billets early evening. The second night I was there, Folkestone was heavily shelled by the Germans from the French coast barely 20 miles away. It was not unlike the Blitz, and I lay in bed convinced that if a shell hit the house it would do so horizontally, and I would ride outside on it — curious because it was nonsense — shells behaved exactly like bombs, coming down vertically. My landlady's husband knocked on my bedroom door and asked me if I would like to join them in the cellar. I was obliged to thank him, but refused because beneath the bedclothes my knees were shaking so badly I didn't think I'd be able to walk! He returned a while later to ask again, adding that his wife needed help with the litter of wee puppy dogs their bitch had given birth to the week before. This worked and I was down like a shot with much greater concern for the adorable pups than myself.

Another evening my friend and I went to the cinema and after the film ended, we had coffee in the cinema café where there was a small dance floor. Some young army officers asked us to dance and joined our table for drinks. It was a lovely summer's evening and they suggested we went for a walk along the cliffs!

Streetwise as we were, we should have known better, but it was our last evening there before returning to Uxbridge and it was by the sea and the young men seemed educated and gentlemanly. I was to learn! We started off along the cliff, gradually breaking off into pairs. Not knowing Folkestone well, we happily walked down a long slope to the lower town — a very different place to the part of town we had been in. There was no one about, it was getting dark and it seemed to consist of several bombed buildings. Obviously it had been an industrial area leading into the docks. I turned round to see if my WAAF friend was behind me, but there was no sign of her. As I did so, the charming and gentlemanly lieutenant pulled me into a derelict building and became very amorous — perhaps lustful would better describe his actions. Luckily I reacted fast, gave him a kick and a shove and ran! By the time I reached the top of the long road up to the main town, I knew I was OK — there were people about and I got on a bus back to my billet — and there was my friend, safely in bed! During the evening we must have told these young men that we were leaving the next day and to our surprise they appeared at the station just as we were boarding the train, apologised for their behaviour, and said goodbye — all part of a learning curve.

Back to Uxbridge and instead of living in the mouse-infested houses, we were billeted in Nissen huts. These were long buildings of various lengths, with a brick-built wall about five feet high and a huge length of corrugated iron placed in a curve over and between the walls. Beds were in rows either side down the length of the 'building' with a circular coke fire in the centre, the smoke going up the black iron flue pipe which went through the corrugated roof. If and when we were able to get a fire going properly, they gave out a good heat and we would boil kettles on the top for tea and hot water bottles. The snag was that the huts were next to a rifle range where rifle practice went on all day, every day — which made sleep impossible during the day following our night watches.

We returned to Uxbridge, back to the Ops Room, where, as 'Y' service operators, we sat next to the Controller on the higher dais. Our radio headsets were connected to the 'Y' service central receiving station at Kingsdown where the translated messages were then passed on to us. We had to watch what was occurring on the Ops table and pass relevant information to the Controller. All this was more difficult when there was a lot of air activity and in particular as most messages referred to places in Germany, names which were strange to us. We had to learn quickly and concentrate intensely. For example, '*Area of bombers (German) now Cologne and*

110

Dusseldorf — spearhead now 20 kilometres south of Cologne.' That was straightforward, but something like *'Allied bombers (British) in the Kaiserslauten area — course 270'* was tricky to spell in a hurry!

Winston Churchill once came to Fighter Command in Uxbridge and left his cigar end behind and it was put in a little glass box. My own prized mementoes of my time in Uxbridge are two notebooks in which as a 'Y' Service operator I had scribbled down the German pilots' translated conversations.

16

Buzz Bombs and Smog

By the summer of 1943, after I had been in the WAAF for nearly two years, Ma wrote and told me they were leaving Lynton. Father had become restless and wanted to be part of the war effort and initially, for a few months, he worked for Shell Mex Oil as an accountant. Poor Ma was sad to leave the Devon countryside and they rented a small flat near Acton Station in London, not a particularly attractive area. His work involved a lot of travelling, so Ma was on her own a lot. I know dear old Grandpa Reynolds visited her frequently from where he was living in Twickenham with her sister, Ellie, and Ellie's husband Charles Kirkwood. On one hilarious Sunday, Grandpa and I roasted a chicken for our lunch as Ma was unwell, but still able to call out instructions from her bedroom. Believe it or not, I had never seen, let alone handled, an uncooked bird before due to my hotel upbringing, and I was loathe to touch the pathetic little corpse. Between us, however, we did produce a tasty meal which, with wartime food rationing, made it particularly special.

I was still stationed at Uxbridge and would go back to be with Ma as much as I could. They only stayed in the flat a few months because Pa kept in touch with friends in the hotel business and was delighted to be offered the position of General Manager of Whitehall Court in Whitehall Place overlooking the river Thames. In those days it was a very large block of service flats — plus a large dining room, lounges

113

and also several well-known London Clubs. Today Whitehall Court is a large hotel — the Royal Horse Guards.

Ma joined the Women's Voluntary Service (WVS), who met round the corner in Trafalgar Square in the crypt of St Martin's in the Field, where they were organised into groups to do book binding. In particular, they repaired prayer books and hymn books which had become very worn and were irreplaceable owing to wartime restrictions. Ma loved doing this work and proudly showed me her uniform — a green overall with 'WVS' embroidered on the breast pocket. She became fond of this part of London with the lovely views of the Thames and the trees along the embankment. She often hummed a popular song of the time which went, 'London Pride is growing again — little pink flowers following the rain.'

But this was also the period when the Germans were again trying to destroy London with the terrifying 'Buzz Bombs' — a type of unmanned missile which flew across the city, very low, making an unpleasant very loud buzzing noise; when the noise stopped, the missile suddenly turned downwards, dropping at random into the city, causing tremendous damage to buildings and much loss of life. Sometimes they were shot down over the sea by the RAF, but not very often, because there was no warning of their approach until the 'buzz' was heard and people didn't have time to take cover in shelters, as had been possible previously during the London Blitz. For many Londoners this caused considerable nervousness and fear and it took Ma a long time to recover from these horrors.

During the winter of 1943, these awful Buzz Bombs were at their worst, but in spite of all the damage and delays I managed to get home to Whitehall Court for my twenty-first birthday in January 1944. Ma had invited two or three of my friends to supper but on that day there was a real 'pea-souper' — extremely dense fog called 'smog'. None of them turned up — the smog had brought almost all transport to a halt. Only the tube trains kept going, which was how I got from Uxbridge to Charing Cross tube station near to Whitehall Court — but guess who was the only other person to arrive? My dear old Grandpa Reynolds (by then eighty), who came on the tube from

114

Twickenham. The smog was so thick that you could hardly see beyond the length of your arm to your hand. Whitehall Court was only a short distance from the tube station and I had to walk slowly, feeling the iron railings on my left until a small light showed the main door. Ma tried very hard to make it a bit of a celebration and the 4 of us had dinner in the main dining room downstairs — there were not many other people there, as the smog and the Buzz Bombs had kept them out of London. It was very much a wartime twenty-first — few cards and presents — £1 from Grandpa (worth a lot of money at that time and more than he could afford). Ma and Pa gave me a beautiful silk scarf which they had managed to buy in Harrods.

Everybody walked a lot in London, using the tube trains for longer journeys — petrol was severely rationed by 1945 and there were very few taxis and buses. Pa's favourite walk was an early evening 'pub crawl' to several of the large London hotels where he sometimes met various acquaintances. If I was at home on leave from the WAAF he liked me to go with him and we would visit the Savoy, the Strand Palace, the Piccadilly, the Ritz, the Dorchester and the Grosvenor. Even if it was difficult for me to persuade him to return home after he had consumed a good deal of alcohol, it certainly widened my knowledge and experience of the hotel world!

During 1944, while our parents were living at Whitehall Court, Peter and I had a lovely holiday down at Lynton. He had just left school and I was on leave from the WAAF. Thanks to Pa's connections in the hotel industry we spent two glorious weeks at the Valley of the Rocks Hotel for free! It was September and with the evenings beginning to draw in, we would dance together after dinner. We were both good dancers, having had ballroom dancing lessons, and thus we thoroughly enjoyed ourselves. Most of the other guests were a good deal older than us and I think they must have enjoyed watching us having such a good time. One evening a bottle of champagne was sent over to our table with the compliments of an elderly couple who apparently thought we were on our honeymoon! I don't think either of us were in the least embarrassed, nor did we explain we were brother and sister — instead, we drank it and went on dancing!

115

Walking with my brother, Peter, on Exmoor

The following morning we went out, up on to Exmoor, riding our two favourite ponies as usual. It was a lovely morning and we were always glad to ride off on our own and not have to be responsible for a group of holiday makers. Eventually we reached our favourite spot for a good gallop, but what we didn't know was that the army had recently positioned an anti-aircraft gun-site nearby where several soldiers were on duty. I suppose these men were pretty bored, stuck there in the middle of nowhere, when they saw Peter and me racing by and they began to shout, egging the ponies on faster. This excited our mounts, who galloped even faster and when we jumped a wide ditch Peter's pony stumbled as it landed and he was thrown off, landing heavily on his shoulder.

When I realised what had happened, I turned my horse around and went back to see if he was all right. He wasn't. He managed to get up on to his feet clutching his shoulder in agony, and he was able to stop his pony taking off by holding on to the reins. With my help he tried to re-mount, but it was impossible. By then we were too far away from the soldiers to call for help, so we walked our ponies to the nearest dry-stone wall and with me pushing him up, he got on to his pony with difficulty. We were several miles from Lynton and he had a rather painful ride back to the stables, particularly going downhill, when every step his pony took jarred his shoulder badly.

After we had returned our ponies to the stables, I took him to the doctor's surgery. The first thing Doctor Nightingale did was to get a large pair of scissors and cut his shirt off. My only thought was how upset Ma would have been, as we were always short of clothing coupons! Poor Peter had broken his collar bone, fortunately a clean break and by the time he had been given some pain-killers, and Doctor Nightingale had strapped up his arm and shoulder securely, we managed to walk back to the hotel and I put him to bed. The following day Peter ate a hearty breakfast and felt much better. After a discussion we decided not to telephone our parents and tell them what had happened to save them worrying and also because we wanted to stay and spend our second week's holiday as planned! Dancing was no longer possible but we still found plenty to do.

When we arrived back at Paddington station, it was dark and we were quite surprised to find a fairly heavy air raid in progress, but we managed to get a taxi to take us to Whitehall Court. You can imagine the horror on our poor parents' faces when we arrived very late at the flat with Peter with his arm in a sling! But we were soon forgiven; they were delighted and relieved at our safe arrival home and our very sensible explanations were happily accepted.

17

100 Group Bomber Command, GIs and Glenn Miller

Some months later all the 'Y' Service team — by then there were eight of us — were posted to 100 Group Bomber Command HQ in Norfolk. We worked in a large country house called Bylaugh Hall, not far from Dereham, and lived in Nissen huts on the estate — in the middle of nowhere, but surrounded by very beautiful countryside.

In Bylaugh Hall there was a large room converted into a drawing office, with wide counters on which there were huge maps of Germany. On the lower floor there was an Ops Room where we worked on night duty and whilst it was not unlike Fighter Command's Ops Room, it was slightly smaller, with a map of Germany showing all the main towns. We were listening out for any information that came back from German aircraft or their ground control station. These were German fighters who would be waiting above certain radio beacons for the British bombers when they had already had some warning that they were coming. The names of these beacons were changed nearly every night, so we had to try and establish where they were, what had been changed and what had not.

When we worked downstairs in the Ops Room very often at night there were only two of us: one corporal and one WAAF officer. I clearly remember the small hours between two and three in the morning when we were tired and there wasn't much happening.

Bylaugh Hall, our base in Norfolk

We often became sleepy and bored; — it was better if you were busy. On one occasion a WAAF officer called Shirley and I were talking — she was only a year or two older than me — and we got around to which schools we had been at. I told her that I lived in Brighton and that I'd been to the High School there and then asked her where she had been. She looked at me and hesitated before saying, 'Well, if you promise not to tell anyone on the station, I was at Roedean.' Of course Roedean was considered to be the crème de la crème and if you were in the Air Force you kept quiet about things like that. I thought it was rather sad.

Trying to keep awake and no doubt drinking endless cups of coffee, we went on chatting about life before the war. She was particularly interested when I described to her how I remembered the regular 'invasions' by the Roedean girls coming to the Grand to spend half-terms with their parents.

120

Whilst I never knew any of them personally, I was always struck by their beautiful and expensive clothes and the total transformation when they changed out of school uniform in their parents' bedrooms. I think I was slightly envious because my own clothes consisted mainly of my bottle-green High School uniform and a few sweaters — all of which were rather drab. All my adult life I've loved and appreciated good quality clothes, probably having been surrounded by so many well-dressed people in the hotel.

Around about this time in Norfolk, I entered a competition in *Vogue* magazine to describe and provide sketches of a suitable selection of outfits for travelling in the form of a 'capsule wardrobe' of clothes. With the help of a friend I put all this together and to my surprise some months later saw in *Vogue* that I was in the list of those who were 'highly commended'!

At Bylaugh, living conditions were slightly better than those we'd experienced at Uxbridge. We were in smaller Nissen huts — sixteen of us — and the ablutions (the toilets and bathrooms) were quite near to us, with plenty of hot water. Somebody, I don't know who, discovered that the tracing paper that we used in the drawing office, which was pale blue linen on metre wide rolls, when soaked in a bath of hot water for long enough was drained of the blue starch, leaving you with pure white cotton. In the days of clothes rationing this was absolutely marvellous, even better than parachute silk, which people used to try and get hold of. Thus we made underclothes and handkerchiefs, Christmas presents and all sorts of things by pinching the blue tracing linen from the drawing office. Having the ablutions nearby was very useful!

I do recall one unpleasant individual at Bylaugh. I was walking across to the mess one morning on my way to breakfast and as I passed the doors at the back there stood the Mess Sergeant ostentatiously doing up his fly front! Being well brought up I averted my eyes and continued quickly into the mess for breakfast. I went straight up to the serving counter at the far end and as I arrived there, the sergeant appeared on the other side of the counter. All of this took a matter of seconds and as I picked up a dish, so the

A group of WAAFs outside our Nissen Hut at East Dereham, Norfolk. Left to right: Barbara, Marguerite, Enid, Ozzie, me

sergeant plunged his hand directly into a very large box of Cornflakes. I realised that he couldn't have had time to wash his hands, so I walked away from the counter with him shouting after me, 'Don't yer want yer Cornflakes?' As it happened, there was to be a mess meeting the same evening and there and then I decided I would go and describe to them what had happened. There were three officers sitting at the top table and only two 'other ranks' in the room besides myself. When it came to the agenda item under which complaints could be raised, I stood up and described the entire incident in detail. The officers appeared impressed with my calm recollections and thanked me, saying that they would investigate the incident immediately.

Needless to say, after this incident the sergeant and I were sworn enemies. On another occasion we were having extremely fatty pork chops for supper which all the WAAF at my table had been complaining about. When the duty officer came round asking if there were any complaints, I was the one, of course, who replied that the chops were inedible. At this, the same sergeant, who was a fat individual, picked up the pork chop off my plate and promptly put it in his mouth, ate it in one gulp and did the same with the chop on the plate of the WAAF next to me. All six of us WAAFs sitting at the table, as well as the young WAAF duty officer, turned somewhat green. A few weeks later, three of us had stayed for a late duty and our Wing Commander rang the Mess to request a late supper. When we entered the Mess this particular sergeant was on duty and initially refused to serve us. Eventually he gave us our supper with very bad grace and when he came to my plate he spat on it. As I turned away I said to him, 'I will make sure that you never get a job in the catering industry!' I ignored whatever he roared back at me.

One of my first adventures in Norfolk, which certainly would not have occurred had I not had the experience of spending my youth in large hotels, took place in the Bell Hotel in Norwich. A few weeks after our arrival at Bylaugh Hall, I and a WAAF friend, Jean, decided we wanted to explore the city of Norwich, about 20 miles away. We hitched in with our gas-mask bags containing our nighties and a toothbrush and the first thing we wanted to do was to book some- where to stay for the night. Much to our surprise the YMCA hostel was full, and all they could suggest was that we go to the police station where they might have a bed. We were horrified!

We then walked further into the centre, which was full of Amer- ican servicemen, past a large hotel on a corner — the Bell. I asked my friend to wait while I went in to see what I could arrange. When the receptionist told me they were full, trying hard not to show how nervous I was, I asked to see the manager, hoping he would be a nice (young) man, like those I had known well who had worked with Pa. To my horror a very tall, large lady dressed in black appeared, wanting to know why I wanted to see her. I took a deep breath and with my best hotel manners, explained that I had been brought up in the hotel business, my father was managing director of the Grand Hotel, Brighton, and I knew that all large hotels keep one or two rooms for emergencies and special guests — and if she had one available, I would be most grateful.

Having looked me up and down and checked back in her office, she announced we could have a room — which proved to be one of the best. I collapsed on the bed in hysterics at what I had achieved — after all, I was only a young WAAF corporal! We laid out our nighties carefully on the beds, placed our toothbrushes in the adjoining bathroom and went out for a meal. The following morning we took it in turns to have a soak in the huge, old-fashioned bath which had a weighted drop-down plug. When it came to Jean's turn she called me to help her as her face flannel had gone down the plug and try as we might, we couldn't extract it. The bath was truly blocked! We felt even guiltier as we made a hasty exit after paying our very reasonable bill as the rather forbidding lady manager had very kindly under-charged us!

My anxiety couldn't have lasted long, however, because I often went back to the Bell and paid for a single room. On one occasion during an air raid, the elderly porter knocked on the door to suggest I should go down to the shelter, but I politely refused — I wasn't going to budge from a bed I had paid for!

At Bylaugh there was a little church near the WAAF site which I rather liked, where services were held for Victory Day and special occasions. I would go there occasionally for the odd prayer. There was an airfield nearby called Swanton Morley and we met a lot of the chaps stationed there because we were taken to dances by bus, or they would come down to a dance at Bylaugh. I met a nice young Welshman called Llewellyn Jones who was very pleasant and had the most beautiful singing voice. We would go off cycling on summer evenings all around the countryside and he would sing while we were cycling, which I loved.

Several things happened on our journeys. Once when we were cycling down the narrow Norfolk lanes we suddenly came upon a field that made us stop and stare. The fields in Norfolk were very much larger than they are in Sussex, about twenty to forty acres — and this particular field, as we looked over a gate, was stacked full with damaged, broken, wrecked aircraft, mainly American bombers, a 'graveyard for planes'. It was a shocking sight; wings were hanging off — obviously they had all been brought on lorries and lifted by cranes and then just dropped in a heap like rubbish. They were stacked, twenty or thirty feet high, one on top of the other, these poor old broken aircraft, and one imagined that there could still be bodies in them. It was a most macabre scene. I have never forgotten it. We stood there just looking at it — I don't know who was more upset, him as a flyer, or me. They had to put the aircraft somewhere, I suppose. What happened to them in the end, I have no idea.

There was another memorable occasion, again on a summer evening. We were sitting on a five-bar gate in the middle of nowhere — no doubt Llewellyn was singing as usual — when suddenly there was a roar of aircraft. Gradually it got louder and louder and we realised that they were all American bombers flying overhead. It was in fact, the very first thousand-bomber daylight raid on Berlin, going out. Something, which the Air Force, knowing a little more about what was going on, had been waiting for. We all wanted to hit back at the Germans to punish them for the dreadful damage to our cities. Seeing this enormous air armada was unbelievable — the sky was totally black with aircraft. I couldn't speak. I remember the tears running down my cheeks thinking that the end of the war was almost in sight. I don't think many people would have seen it because almost all the big American airbases were in East Anglia and they would have gone out straight over the coast.

During the time I was in Norfolk the WAAFs at Bylaugh were often invited to dances at the American bases, but on one occasion we went to a camp full of New Zealanders. It was the first visit by the RAF and WAAFs and only about 12 of us went. I think it was arranged this way because the New Zealanders had only recently arrived in the country and were still a somewhat unknown factor. What a wise arrangement this proved to be.

We arrived in a large hall a short time after we had been told to, but it was almost empty except for a few men arranging chairs and tables. We sat down together round a table and waited. Eventually a few men came in and the bar was opened, the dance band began to play and a large group of women arrived, some in uniform and some civilians — probably girls from nearby villages. We continued to sit but nobody came over to us so one or two of the RAF men got up and went to the bar to buy us drinks and brought them back to our table. As the hall filled up we joined in the dancing, but only WAAFs with RAF as no on else spoke to us. After a while we WAAFs were asked to dance by the New Zealanders. I had a couple or so dances with quite a nice man, who was a good dancer. It was a very warm summer's evening and it got very hot in the hall, so my partner suggested we went to stand outside the main entrance to get a bit of fresh air. Then he began to walk down a path away from the hall, and suddenly, while he was still talking, he grabbed hold of me roughly, pulling me towards a gap in the hedge. With some difficulty I managed literally to fight him off and run back to the hall. When I joined my own party they showed their concern as I was feeling pretty frightened. Minutes later a group of New Zealanders, including the one who had tried to molest me, approached our table and he tried to grab my arm, shouting, 'this is the one, she led me on,' calling me names like 'dirty floozy', 'tart' and 'whore'. At that point two of the RAF sergeants got up, stood in front of me and told the by then large group of New Zealanders to go away and leave us but they turned very unpleasant and began to lash out with their fists. Fortunately, the Military Police were standing nearby and they came over and intervened, removing the New Zealanders, most of whom had been drinking very hard. The hall was cleared, and an announcement made that the dance had been concluded. We were then escorted by the Military Police back to our bus and went home to Bylaugh!

This was a very unpleasant experience and I and the other five WAAFs did not go out to many more dances. Strangely enough the men who seemed to want to cause trouble were mainly the colonials — Australians, Canadians and New Zealanders. We never encountered any unpleasantness at any of the many American bases we went to, except when we had our bicycles stolen — but more about that later!

We had the opportunity of meeting quite a lot of Americans because we were bussed down to the American bases to go to their dances. They were extremely well behaved; far better than the Australians or the New Zealanders. I think there was more discipline. On one occasion in early December 1944, about ten of us — five WAAFs and five RAF chaps — cycled down to Attleborough, a huge

126

American airbase about 10 miles south of Bylaugh. It was a very special evening because Glenn Miller, the American band leader, was going to be there. Even then he was very famous. When we arrived we were taken to one of the enormous hangars built to accommodate the huge bombers. The circular roof of the hangar was supported by great iron rafters which had holes in them — rather like Meccano. I would guess that the whole thing was around a hundred yards wide. Sitting astride these beams were lots of American airmen. There was a stage with a large dance band on it — there was no actual dancing, we just listened to the music. Glenn Miller sang and played and the concert must have lasted two or three hours. The following week he was flying out to Paris to entertain the troops, and it was on that trip that he was lost and believed killed over the sea. His body was never found.

In 1944, towards the end of the war, the second boyfriend who I remember well when I was stationed at Bylaugh was a Canadian pilot from Montreal called Jerry who was blond, blue-eyed and rather attractive. We became good friends but there was a slightly complicated incident when he came up to the drawing office and said that he had booked rooms for us to go away for the weekend. This was something I had never done before, but he had booked *two* rooms in Cambridge at a hotel called the University Arms. I was rather flattered and not in the least worried and quite excited. I thought this sounded fun and looked forward to the following weekend. The next day, however, I received a letter from my mother telling me that Sir James and Lady Garner — who had lived in the Grand for almost all of my childhood (and whose grandson I eventually married) — were now living at the University Arms Hotel in Cambridge! So I had to tell poor Jerry that there was no way I could go!

Unfortunately all this was overheard by one of the WAAFs who I had mistakenly believed to be a good friend. When I got back to the hut, there was a note on my bed saying, 'I've been in touch with Jerry, and I'm going to Cambridge with him.' I was so furious that I picked up a large book and with great force threw it from one end of the hut to the other. Suffice it to say that was the end of our friendship and I don't know what happened to Jerry.

Another unfortunate incident occurred in the ablutions one day when a bee stung my bottom. Of course the ablutions were not exactly open air but I don't think that the roof actually fitted down on to the wall, so while it stopped the rain there was a gap for hygiene purposes. I know we were used to the rain blowing in, and that was most uncomfortable, but the bee sting was worse!

Not too far away from Bylaugh was a gravel pit where we often went swimming, which was fun, even if it was very deep, cold and rather dangerous. Another interesting place I visited, called Gorlestone, was very secret — it was in the middle of Yarmouth, right on the harbour's edge. I was taken there by Shirley, who asked me if I wanted a trip out on the condition that I musn't say anything to anybody and I must be very careful as it was hush hush. It was in fact the base for the mini-submarines which eventually attacked the *Tirpitz*; these were very small submarines with only two men in them. We saw all these strange-looking craft lined up in the harbour, presumably prior to their top-secret mission.

I met all kinds of people when I was in the services. One day I was hitching into Norwich when I got into a car with a mother and daughter, a very charming pair who, it turned out, were the owners of a mink farm nearby. The daughter was working with her mother because it was a reserved occupation. They told me how the aircraft were causing them a great deal of anxiety because the noise frightened all their breeding minks, causing them to abort. I went down there for a meal occasionally and they were nice people. Sometime later when I was back in London, I went with a friend to have dinner at the Regent Palace Hotel, when who should walk in draped with mink coats but this mother and daughter, which was quite extraordinary and most impressive.

We did lots of cycling in Norfolk because it was flat and the RAF supplied us with bicycles. We would regularly go to the farms near Bylaugh Hall, where we could buy butter. It was rationed and this was beautiful farm butter. We would then go in to the local bakery,

Sunning myself before a swim at the chalk pits near Bylaugh Hall. Friends told me that I looked like Bette Davis in this photo; I had a 23" waist at the time

which was actually an old-fashioned mill where they ground the wheat into flour and baked the bread as well. We would buy these beautiful fresh loaves with wonderful crusts and break off the crusts and eat them while we cycled because we were usually starving. We would also be able to get eggs, which we could cook in our Nissen huts in a frying pan on the top of the funny old stove in the centre of the hut. So we got tomatoes and other bits and had a jolly good fry-up, which made a nice change from the food in our mess.

There was another occasion when a group of us (from the RAF and WAAF) were invited to the big American airbase at Attleborough and we cycled over during the evening. On our arrival we were told by the American guards to leave our bikes in a field. We were stunned to see hundreds of bikes in this huge field. Thinking we were rather clever, we decided to chain our bikes up and leave them in the next field behind a hedge and went off to the dance. I remember meeting a rather nice American called Hank who was from the 'Deep South' — better spoken than most Americans and of course (with my hotel upbringing) I was a bit of a snob! We had fun, not only dancing ourselves, but also watching the Americans jiving — the latest dance craze which had hit the States. At around midnight the band stopped playing and we slowly made our way back to the field to find our bikes ... only to find not a bike was in sight — not one! Every single bike had disappeared from both the large field and where we had left ours in the adjoining one.

My nice American was very sympathetic and invited us to back to the mess and he arranged for transport to take us back to Bylaugh. We went with him and on the way there were fascinated to see loads of GIs wearing baseball caps back-to-front — we had never seen headgear like it before — and pushing massive, three-foot-wide brooms around to clean up the hangar. At about 2 a.m. we had another new experience, when everyone downed tools to eat pork chops with apricot jam — an extraordinary but enjoyable meal! A little later, in the early hours, we were all taken back to camp in two cars. We heard later that the Americans were in the habit of taking bikes whenever they wanted one, wherever they happened to be — and when they had reached their destination, would dump them in the nearest ditch or village pond. When Pa found out, he was not impressed as it was my own, personal bike, and after that I was relegated to a free RAF bone-shaker!

Near to the WAAF site, just beyond the estate perimeter, was a working gravel pit. The lorries took away gravel, mostly used as the base beneath the tarmac of landing strips at the airfields which by then covered Norfolk — both RAF and American bases. The WAAFs and RAF men would use the lorries rather like a free taxi service to give us all a lift to the main road between Fakenham and Norwich. From there we hitchhiked into Norwich and then many of us hitched all the way to London when we had a 72 hour pass, or three days' leave. This was much easier than it sounds. Whilst there were not many private civilian cars, there were plenty of lorries and service vehicles. I have always believed that being in uniform was a safe-guard and I never had any trouble. All of the drivers were pleasant and helpful and usually pleased to have company on long, lonely journeys.

On the few occasions when I took a chance without having a leave pass and I hitched to London, I discovered that I was less likely to be stopped by the Military Police if I entered via the East End, than if I went in via the West End, where my parents were living in Whitehall.

On one occasion I returned to camp quite late in the day. It was during the summer and I must have got into Norwich station at about 9 o'clock in the evening. I had a twenty-mile hitchhike to get back to camp. I got a bus to the outskirts of the city, where I then hoped to get a lift, so I started walking, knowing I had a long way to go. There was very little traffic and I kept walking until finally an army motorcyclist came by and he stopped and offered me a lift. However, I was terrified of motorbikes and politely declined. He said, 'You won't get a lift as late as this.' I still refused. He continued on his own and I continued walking. A couple of miles further on he had stop-ped to wait for me and said, 'I told you, you won't get a lift.' This time I agreed and I got on, clutching him around the middle, noticing the smell of his khaki and uniform. I said, 'I'll only get on if you promise that if a car or a lorry comes by you'll let me get off.' He promised, he was a decent sort. We went quite a long way and finally a lorry did come by and he stopped and I climbed in — much to my relief — and arrived safely back in camp at last! Being very late, I crawled in under the wire and made my way to the Nissen hut.

Only once did I and a friend have a real scare when hitchhiking. We were waiting in a remote country road for a car to come by, when in the distance we saw a convoy of army trucks coming towards us. Fortunately I have very long sight and I suddenly realised that I could not see the drivers' faces because they were black! Both of us dived into the roadside ditch to hide and the large convoy of trucks — all full of black American soldiers — passed us by. At that

131

time we had not yet become accustomed to the large numbers of black GIs who had begun to arrive from the States!

All kinds of things happened in those days. One evening I went up to the drawing office to go on night duty and my friend Ozzie who was a sergeant, said, 'Stay in the outer office — we are having a crisis in the map room.' There were several people going in and out but I had no idea what was happening. Later it transpired that another WAAF, a very attractive Irish girl, was having a miscarriage and they thought I was too young and innocent to be helpful!

Outside the front entrance and drawing office of 100 Group Bomber Command, Bylaugh Hall with fellow WAAFS — I am on the far right

Several of the WAAFs in my group were married while at Bylaugh Hall. Ozzie married a very nice American doctor called Herb, short for Herbert. After the war they went to America and lived in North Dakota, right up in the wilds near the Canadian border and they had

132

six children. Herb worked for a medical practice, partially funded by the state department. Some years later he was asked to leave the practice because it was considered he was treating too many Indians! He had a great interest in the native Americans and their well-being because they had been so badly treated by the white American settlers. Ozzie and I still keep in touch, exchanging Christmas cards and small presents — which is remarkable, 60 years later.

Now, there isn't a great deal more to tell about Bylaugh except that I did return there after the war with my husband Frank, son Robin and daughter Linda, then about 9 and 7 years old, to show them where I'd been during the war. To their absolute delight, and which they have never forgotten, the Nissen hut which I lived in was being used by the local farmer and was full of pigs!

18

Colkirk, North Norfolk

And now for Colkirk, a very special place, a large working farm belonging to the Joice family. But before telling you all about the family and the farm, I will begin with a little story which really has a 'wow factor' and whet your appetite for more! Imagine a lovely sunny day when Joan Joice and I, together with her children Roger and Sallie, aged four and two, were outside in the drive in front of the very old farmhouse. Just behind where we standing was a large barn and a telephone cable stretched between the top of the barn and chimney on top of the farmhouse roof — hardly more than forty feet above our heads. Suddenly we heard and saw a Mosquito fighter bomber aircraft coming in very low across the fields towards us. Almost before Joan and I realised what was happening, the pilot had flown *under* the cable between the farmhouse and barn. He then turned back slowly towards us, did a Victory roll (rolling the whole plane over) and waved down towards us. He was gone as suddenly as he had come.

Roger and Sallie were crying and Joan and I were speechless with surprise and shock. When she could speak, Joan was absolutely furious, saying, 'How dare he do it? He could have hit the house and killed us all!' — which of course was perfectly true. She knew who he was — a young pilot whom she had heard talking about doing it the previous night at a party — there were always parties when the RAF chaps came over from West Raynham air base.

As we sat drinking tea in the large kitchen, having calmed down

135

the frightened children, Joan said, 'Wait 'til Jack comes home, he must report it to the RAF authorities.' Whilst I am sure Joan did tell Jack that evening, I heard no more about it. Jack probably persuaded Joan to forget the incident. He would have explained that these very young flying types were all daredevils to one degree or another — otherwise they could not have been able to do the job that was expected of them, risking their lives over Germany day after day in defence of our country. But this did make them great fun at all the parties!

Back to how I happened to be at Colkirk. One day when a friend and I were hitchhiking into Norwich we were given a lift by Jack and Joan Joice. They were very friendly and kind and invited us to Colkirk for a weekend party. For me this was the start of a special friendship which lasted many years and of which I have very happy memories, precious to this day. Several years later, Jack became my son Robin's godfather.

Colkirk was a large farm a few miles south of Fakenham. Between them, the Joice family — father Charlie and two sons, Jack and Dick — farmed a very large part of north Norfolk. Farming was a very vital part of the war effort — food production was essential because so many of our ships bringing us supplies from the USA and Canada were being sunk by the German U-boats (submarines). Thus Jack, as a farmer, was in a 'reserved occupation' (he developed a bit of a complex because he was unable to join up — he would love to have been in the RAF as a flier). Raynham Farm, next to Colkirk, was commandeered by the RAF and became a large airfield; hence, another part of Jack and Joan's war effort was to give as much pleasure as possible to the men stationed there and Colkirk became a kind of escape and a second home for many of the chaps — mainly pilots.

When the aircrews came to Colkirk, mainly from West Raynham, they usually came in small groups, and seldom referred to the war — never mentioning the loss of aircraft or the failure of friends to return home to base following recent operations. These young men flew Mosquito planes — long-range fighter and observation aircraft that went ahead of the main group of bombers, dropping flares down to indicate the target areas. They were a very close-knit bunch of friends and the visits to Colkirk were important to them, a haven where they could temporarily forget the horrors of the war. Their arrival was always greeted with great pleasure by Jack, Joan, Roger and Sallie, to be followed by a drink sitting in a comfortable armchair by a roaring log fire.

Meals at Colkirk were always fabulous (in spite of rationing), not only because Joan was a very good cook, but, as with most farms, there was always a large joint of meat — a pig or a sheep having conveniently dropped dead — plenty of home-grown veg and fruit and of course eggs, cream and butter. On a Sunday when there was a joint of beef, before Jack began to carve it, Roger and Sallie (and no doubt also Nigel and Christopher the two younger sons a few years later) would stand either side of their father's chair whilst he tipped the carving dish a little, causing the blood gravy to run onto a large spoon which he then fed into the children's mouths. Sometimes if there was a lot of blood, it was then given to any young visitors, like myself, with the words, 'This will build you up to fight the war!'

On one particular evening I was upstairs giving little Sallie her bath, which we both enjoyed, and after I had sprinkled on some scented talcum powder and put on her nightie she insisted on going downstairs to kiss all the boys goodnight. We went down the old winding wooden stairs that led directly into the sitting room where several young men were comfortably sprawled in large armchairs, drinking beer and waiting for supper — the cosy and homely atmosphere was much appreciated and they all loved to make a fuss of the children. Sallie was the prettiest little thing, with blonde curls and blue eyes, and after she had kissed them all goodnight, and no doubt to prolong the occasion, she lifted up her nightie and said, 'Smell my tummy, I've got lots of Auntie Pam's special powder on me.' Several obliged and then they all chorused, much to my embarrassment, 'We would rather smell Auntie Pam's tummy!!' I hurried Sallie upstairs to bed.

In the evening we would play the silliest games imaginable; for example, the girls would go out of the room where they were blindfolded, guided back in and then told that they were to kneel down and put one hand into a bowl to find a silver coin. This was done with ceremony and laughter because when the coin was found the blindfold was removed, and one was gazing down into a large old-fashioned chamber pot containing lemonade and an uncooked pork sausage — and you can guess what we immediately thought it was!

Sometimes several RAF chaps would stay the night if we partied late and Joan would slip away during the evening to make up beds upstairs. The men slept three or four in a room and the WAAFs together in the next room. It was very like boarding school, especially when the young men came into the girls' dormitory, jumping from bed to bed whilst we made ourselves as small as possible to avoid being jumped upon. Eventually Joan came in and shooed them back to their own beds, rather like a jolly school matron!

Jack Joice was a special sort of person, always tremendous fun, very kind and generous, and I even got used to being in the Land Rover with him when he would suddenly brake to a stand still, grab his gun from the back seat and shoot rabbits, then jump out and run and collect them for supper! The first time it happened I was taken by surprise being a 'town girl', but it is amazing what you can get used to!

Teasing was also his forte. He often took the family, including his young sister, Betty, younger than me, to Brancaster Sands on the coast for picnics. On one occasion it suddenly turned very hot and Betty and I were moaning because we had not taken our swimsuits. 'Don't worry,' said Joan, 'go in wearing your pants and bras.' We hesitated but as the sands were completely deserted we agreed. Jack behaved very well, for him, discreetly looking away while we stripped off our outer clothes, little knowing what was in his mind! The sea was beautiful and we both enjoyed a lovely swim. As we waded out of the shallow water, Joan was standing, with Jack nearby, at the water's edge holding out two small towels she had found in the car. As we both stepped forward to take a towel, Joan stepped quickly backwards and kept the towel out of our reach, meanwhile, Jack produced a camera and was snapping us like mad! Eventually we grabbed a towel each and got dressed over our wet undies — oh, such modesty!

Two or three weeks later during a very relaxed evening partying with several RAF types I noticed Jack was handing round something which caused great hilarity and Joan was 'tut-tutting' to him a bit. Various comments from all became more and more personal. Finally I was allowed to see what it was all about: several photos of Betty and me walking out of the sea with our arms outstretched (for the towels!), apparently absolutely naked! Apparently when we went in the sea, Jack had rushed to get his camera because we were both wearing nylon pants and bras, which had become transparent as we emerged from the water. How we both blushed when the young men refused to hand the snaps back and put them in their pockets. So perhaps a photo of Betty and me was flown over Berlin — let's hope it brought luck to the boys!

Besides myself, there were only two other WAAFs who also went over to Colkirk — but we always went alone, as the other two would be on duty. Colkirk was about 10 miles north of Bylaugh Hall, near to the north Norfolk market town of Fakenham. During the summer months I usually cycled through several hamlets and along narrow lanes to get there. It was often very hot and I never saw a car, only an occasional farm tractor.

Colkirk was certainly among my happiest wartime memories. One other memory is of the long impromptu discussions held in the drawing office on the first floor at Bylaugh Hall. Various RAF young men would come in whilst we drank endless cups of tea and coffee and discussed politics, the war and everything else under the sun, but mostly planned for the future, both individual and national. I think we all believed that politicians had made a real mess of our lives so far!

While I was stationed in Norfolk, I could not get home as often as I had done when I was Uxbridge. I don't think any of us were actually homesick, however, probably because we were kept very busy —

but we did sometimes miss 'home comforts' — particularly during the cold winter months. It was at this time that my dear Ma sometimes sent me a 10-shilling note (now 50 pence), which went towards some new stockings or a meal out, as well as regular small parcels of goodies — often in shoeboxes! They contained things like biscuits or the odd small bar of chocolate, some hankies, a little jar of marmalade and, occasionally, magazines — all of which I treasured, knowing that Ma had gone without her sweet ration — so I wrote to her as often as I could telling her about the lovely countryside, Colkirk, and the girls I worked with. Of course, mentioning the work we did was not allowed as it was all very top secret.

Eventually I took my riding clothes back to camp with me as I was able to go riding with Betty, Jack's younger sister. The first time this happened I was in a dilemma. I had been invited by my Canadian boyfriend to go with him and a group of friends all the way to London and then on to Epsom to see the Derby — one of the few national events which re-started towards the end of the war. I was very torn between the two invitations, but Testerden won, and I had a wonderful weekend with Betty and her parents. Testerden was an even larger farm than Colkirk where horses were still used for ploughing — huge, gentle, hard-working shires — sadly, soon to be replaced by tractors.

I clearly remember Betty and myself going for a long ride when we both got drenched with rain and on our return, Mrs Joice (Jack's mother) took us straight up to Betty's bedroom where she had lit a lovely coal fire. She insisted we stripped all our clothes off and wrapped us in huge warm bath towels. She then dried our hair with another warm towel. When we were completely dry and dressed in fresh dry clothes, we had a large sherry each before a super hot meal with Mr and Mrs Joice in the large dining room. Most of all it is the feeling of being so kindly and beautifully 'mothered' I remember so well — so special after the pretty bleak conditions of service life.

After the war Betty Joice was married to a young man who worked on the Sandringham estate, where they lived in a cottage for several years. Betty later told me lovely stories about old Queen Mary, the grandmother to our present Queen Elizabeth, who liked to be driven around the vast estate in her large, old-fashioned Rolls-Royce car. If she felt in need of a cup of tea she would tell the chauffeur to stop outside any of the tenants' cottages, and he was then sent to alert them that 'Her Majesty is coming to visit you'. The unexpected element was unnerving, especially to the new and younger wives. To cap it all, Betty told me how the Queen would pass a gloved finger over the polished furniture before sitting down, invariably saying, 'Betty dear, you have not dusted today.' The old lady then expected a large tea of cucumber sandwiches and cream cakes. After the first visit most of the wives tried to be prepared, but it was not easy as the visits were always impromptu, so unless the weather was very bad they had to be ready!

My time at Bylaugh came to an end when I was posted back to Uxbridge in the September of 1945, the war in Europe having come to an end in May 1945.

A few weeks before I left Bylaugh an extremely bizarre event took place. One morning, the Wing Commander came into the Drawing Office and told us he was having some special visitors that afternoon. He explained that several high-ranking German Luftwaffe officers had been brought over from Germany so they could be cross-examined by their counterparts in the RAF on highly secret and technical matters concerning the 'Y' service. He said that we would be expected to serve them with tea in the Wing Commander's office. There were only three of us on duty that day and whilst we were all utterly astonished at this particular turn of events, orders were orders, and whatever our private feelings were, we had to obey. Two of us took a tray with tea and biscuits in and when the bell rang a second time, I went in, and was told that the two RAF officers and three Luftwaffe officers would all like a second cup. The Germans were all tall men in uniform who stood up and clicked their heels as I entered the room. I had the impression that they were anxious to appear well-mannered.

Needless to say, we three girls were overwhelmed by the event — it seemed quite extraordinary that were serving tea to Germans who only a few weeks previously had been trying to defeat the British, and the British to defeat the Germans. A little later we looked out of the window and saw the Germans leaving in two large cars with an armed escort. Afterwards Wing Commander Wells came into the office and thanked us for cooperating and gave us various German medals and badges which had been left for us by the visitors. None of us ever found out any details of what information had been given, and nothing more was ever heard about the incident. It was all rather strange and we felt somewhat indignant that we had been expected to serve tea to German officers!

On an altogether happier note, around the same time, several of us gave Jack and Joan Joice tea in our Nissen hut. When Jack heard that the WAAFs who had visited Colkirk were soon leaving, he told me his ambition was to see inside the hut we lived in. It had to be arranged very carefully as of course civilians were not allowed into the camp. Our hut was on the edge of the WAAF site and near to the wire fence, which we girls often crawled under if we were going off camp without a pass, but we had to be very careful as it was near to where the RAF men were guarding a side entrance to camp.

With great care we smuggled Jack and Joan in under the wire and into our hut, where we gave them tea. Joan was worried we would be in trouble if anyone else came in and saw them, but we had a plan for such an event — we had another WAAF on lookout from the hut window and we were going to shut them both in the hut loo if anyone appeared! Jack thoroughly enjoyed himself, meeting other WAAFs, seeing our 'bed-spaces' and looking at photographs of friends and family. His laughter was infectious and everyone enjoyed the visit, but we did heave a sigh of relief when we managed to get them out again safely under the wire fence — quite a challenge as Jack was a large, plumpish man! It was almost dark by the time they left and they had to walk quite a way to their car which had been left at the end of the lane.

A few weeks after Jack and Joan's visit to the Nissen hut, I was quite suddenly posted back to 11 Group HQ at Uxbridge. Leaving so many good friends and a part of the country I had learned to love was sad, but by then many of the personnel at Bylaugh had left, the war had been over for two months and we no longer had much work to do.

Being back in Uxbridge was depressing. It was an ugly place on the edge of London and at the end of the underground train line. By this time I was getting aches and pains in my chest and was very tired. I seemed to spend a lot of time seeing doctors at the RAF hospital, a large place on the edge of the camp. I was back working in the drawing office of air traffic control, above ground thankfully, with not much work to do. The only work I did of any significance was to copy out various large complicated plans for the future air-port at nearby Heathrow. The medics asked me if I would like to sleep at home as I was sleeping so badly. Naturally I jumped at the idea, and for a couple of months or so, commuted back and forth to Whitehall Court. This turned out to be not such a good idea as I was spending two and a half hours a day travelling on the tube trains — one and a quarter hours in the morning to Uxbridge and one and a quarter hours back to Whitehall in the evening. When I arrived home mother realised there was something wrong with me. I was so exhausted I could hardly walk, and she put me straight to bed and brought me my supper.

I was at Uxbridge for another 3 months before I was invalided out with nervous exhaustion just before Christmas 1945, with my final discharge date being 8 February 1946. Too much night duty had taken its toll and it was a while before I recovered — a somewhat depressing and lonely conclusion to my service career which I had enjoyed so much. But I had served a total of five years with the WAAF and was ready to move on to the next phase of my life.

R.A.F. FORM 1394.

ROYAL AIR FORCE.

BRIEF STATEMENT OF SERVICE AND CERTIFICATE OF DISCHARGE OF

The corner of this certificate to be cut off if the airman/airwoman is discharged with a "bad" character, or with disgrace or if specially directed by the Air Council.

SURNAME.....SIDNEY-SMITH,.....Official No.....2066191

Christian Names.....PAMELA

Date of enlistment ~~enrolment~~ .....2.9.41.....Terms of enlistment ~~enrolment~~ .....D.P.E.

(a) Date reported for regular service.....30.10.41

(b) Branch of Air Force in which enlisted.....W.A.A.F......R.A.F. trade on discharge.....Clerk S.D.

Date of discharge.....8.2.46.....Rank on discharge.....Corporal

(c) Cause of discharge.....K.R. & A.C.I.para.652(22) - Services no longer required.

(Para......652.....Clause.....22....King's Regulations and Air Council Instructions.)

(d) General character (i) during service.....Very Good......(ii) on discharge.....Very Good.

(e) Degree of trade proficiency :—A .....Satisfactory......B.....Satisfactory.

Special qualifications.....Nil.

(f) Medals, Clasps, Decorations, Mentions in Despatches, Special Commendations, etc ..... Nil.

DESCRIPTION OF ABOVE-NAMED AIRMAN/AIRWOMAN ON DISCHARGE.

Date of birth .....15.1.23.....Marks or scars .....Nil.

Height.....Five.....ft.....Seven.....ins.

Complexion.....Fresh.

Colour of eyes.....Brown......Colour of hair.....

Airman's or airwoman's signature .....

(g) Brief statement of any special aptitudes or qualities or any special types of employment for which recommended :—

Cpl. Sidney-Smith has been employed with the Air Traffic Centre during the last five months and has always carried out her duties most satisfactorily. A conscientious and hardworking N.C.O.

Unit Date Stamp [MINISTRY (UNIT) ... 14 DEC 1945 ROYAL AIR FORCE]

(Signed) .....S/Ldr., Admin.

for Off. Commanding .....Air Ministry Unit.

Royal Air Force.

Attention is directed to Notes (a) to (g) on reverse.

My discharge papers from the RAF

19

Post-war Years — The Grand Re-opens

The Grand Hotel was returned by the military authorities to the owners, Spiers and Ponds, in the late autumn of 1945, when there was a short ceremony involving the handing back of the keys to my father by several high- ranking officers on the front steps. I think the military must have started to move out some weeks earlier, as there was still a great deal of repair and refurbishment to be done. Pa was very upset to see the dreadful state the hotel was in. The Australians who had been stationed there seemed to have been hell-bent on causing as much mindless destruction as possible.

Sadly, the beautiful stairwell had been horribly misused by drunken soldiers who, in the early days, threw their 'mates' over the balustrade from the upper floors and who fell over a hundred feet and were killed immediately. As soon as possible the army authorities had heavy wire netting put across from one side to the other at all six levels.

The Australians seemed to have been both barbaric and destructive. Before finally leaving they deliberately destroyed all they could, pulling out fittings — basins, baths, toilets, taps, pipes, curtain rails and even doors off hinges — and doing as much damage as they were able. Was it all due to drink and high spirits? I don't think so; it seems probable some of these men were descendants of the original convicts sent out to Australia and held a deep-seated anger towards the country of their origin.

The good that came as a result of the damage was a large amount of compensation money paid by the Australian government, which allowed a complete refurbishment of the whole hotel. When it was re-opened nearly a year later it was even better and more beautiful than it had been before the war. Coincidentally much of the work was carried out by an old established Brighton-based building company, F.T. Wilson & Sons of St James Street — which I married into in 1949 and, following the early death of my husband Frank Wilson in 1969, I became chairman of the company for twenty years.

My father being handed back the key to the Grand Hotel at the end of World War Two, by a group of Air Force officers

Ma, Pa and I returned to live in the Grand in the early spring of 1946. This time we occupied a large suite on the first floor facing the sea, consisting of two bedrooms, a large bathroom and a large sitting room. Brother Peter was still in the Navy, only coming home on brief leave visits before going to Reading University to study agriculture, as he had always wanted to be a farmer.

Brighton was bleak and windy after my happy time in Norfolk, where it always seemed to be summer! There were shortages of fuel and food and rationing was still in force. I remember that the first bananas to be seen since the beginning of the war appeared in Brighton in early 1946 and local housewives became very angry about flour and bread still being in short supply in the summer of that year. It was reported in the local newspapers that thousands of local women had signed petitions in revolt against the rationing schemes announced by the Ministry of Food. I think we were fortunate to be living in the hotel, because I don't recall many discomforts.

By then Father was working furiously hard towards reopening the Grand. Some of the old staff had returned, but sadly many did not. Several young men had lost their lives in the war, so many new staff had to be found and engaged. Several of the newcomers were Italians, strange when you think about it, as Italy had fought against us on the side of the Germans during the very recent war. But they were very popular with guests and staff, charming and very well mannered and I recall two men in particular.

First, Nico Sonvicco, a tall handsome man, who flirted with all the ladies, who became the maître d'hôtel, the restaurant manager and head waiter. Mrs Marlow was particularly fascinated by him, and encouraged him and flirted with him outrageously, which they both enjoyed. Then, providing Sonvicco wasn't around, she would mimic him, particularly his rather distinctive and graceful arm movements as he walked whilst showing guests to their tables in the dining room, when the flourishes became quite wild.

The other man was Silvanno Trompetto, who became head chef but he was only at the Grand a few years. He was so good at his job that he was 'stolen' from the Grand to become head chef at the Savoy Grill at the Savoy Hotel in London. Many years later I stayed there with my second husband, Kenneth, who rushed off to a meeting as soon as we arrived, so I was left to my own devices. I telephoned down to the kitchens to find out if Trompetto was still there and much to my delight he was! He promptly came to the phone and invited me to go down and see the kitchens. After our

147

tour we went into his office and had several glasses of very expensive champagne. He had a somewhat strange appearance due to a car accident when his face was badly damaged and his nose completely squashed. This did not put him off his obsession with racing cars and there was an interesting series of television programmes all about him and his collection of classic sports cars. I have a piece of engraved silver that he gave to my father when he left.

Following my demobilization, a grateful government generously gave me £40 gratuity to help me start out in Civvy Street. I couldn't wait to buy some new civilian clothes, having spent the best part of five years in uniform. I went along the seafront to a very special shop near the Old Ship Hotel called Barrance and Fords, and bought myself the most beautiful pale blue coat costing £25. It had a high collar and was waisted with a tie belt above a flared skirt which was just below my knees, and I felt like the cat's whiskers in it. At the same time, I bought a pair of small clip-on earrings in the shape of pink flowers, which I rather liked. The euphoria of making my purchases was promptly deflated by my mother, who was appalled that I should spend so much on a coat — she said she had never spent more than £12 on one and she thought that the earrings were common! (One of Ma's favourite homilies, indeed, was, 'Women who think too much about clothes are considered scarlet women'!) Her attitude really upset me and I made a vow that if I had a daughter of my own, I would never criticise any clothes which she bought — even if I didn't like them.

All his life Pa had enjoyed parties, plus a bit of gambling. Soon after the reopening of the hotel, he was invited to a party in a large house at the lower end of Grand Avenue, Hove. As Mother did not want to go, he took me and it turned out to be quite an exciting event. Many of the so-called crème de la crème of Brighton and Hove were there — mayors and aldermen; local businessmen; the odd Member of Parliament or two; plus a sprinkling of titled individuals. Greeted by our host and hostess, we were given glasses of fine champagne and began to circulate and talk to people my father knew. Whilst standing in the large drawing room, my attention was focused on a very fine and unusual oil painting of colourful flowers. It had been framed into a panel about eight feet long and one foot deep and was built into the huge carved mantelpiece — stretching across the wall above a large log fire. It was an unusual and eye-catching feature in an impressive and lovely room and I have always remembered it.

In one room a roulette game had been set up and in another, baccarat. Both games were in full swing and large amounts of pound notes were on each table. After a lavish buffet supper, carpets were removed and a small dance floor appeared. Nearing midnight I was dancing, when suddenly Pa appeared and almost grabbed me away from my partner, saying, 'We must leave immediately.' He barely gave me time to find my coat and hurried me out of a side door, where several other guests were also scurrying out.

His car was parked nearby and as we drove away, three or four police cars arrived and policemen ran into the house! Fortunately, a friend had tipped Pa off that a police raid was imminent — not really surprising, as gambling on such a large scale was considered illegal even in private houses! I have always wanted to know who our hosts were!

After the war Brighton was a town of extreme contrasts, with a number of wealthy individuals, but also many very poor families living in appalling slum conditions. Indeed, certain areas of East Brighton such as Albion Hill had no electricity until the middle of the 1950s. At that time our gardener's wife was making gas mantles (little net covers for gas lamps), and selling them, twenty-five for a shilling (5 pence today). Some of the extremes of poverty and wealth are impossible to imagine today.

After I had been back in Brighton a few weeks, a friend of Pa offered me a job as secretary with a small commercial art firm called Design Projects. There were three artists, Stuart, Brian and John, and there was me — a hopeless secretary. All kinds of artwork was undertaken — none of which paid very well, however, and we closed down at the end of the first year. During that time we did some weird and wonderful murals in elaborate gold-leaf decoration at the top of the columns in the Grand Hotel banqueting room. We painted something similar at the King Alfred Sports Centre, very large and attractive sea views of Brighton in the restaurant on the Palace Pier, and a huge mural in Regency style in English's fish restaurant — where the chaps painted the faces of their wives or girl-friends. This was still there a few years ago, but much altered.

While I was at Design Projects, the winter of 1946–1947 was one of the worst since the winter that postponed the start of the war. The blizzards started to arrive about a week after my birthday in January. The whole of Sussex became icebound, buses and trolley-buses in Brighton halted, milkmen delivered milk on sledges and hundreds of people queued for coal. This dreadful weather, coming so soon after the end of the war, caused much suffering. Even the sea froze in places and there were so many accidents that police cars were used as ambulances. There is often a lighter side to life, however, and in the midst of all this hardship, I remember reports that the wartime habit of eating ice cream all year round (brought over from America by the GIs) had caught on, and new ice-cream parlours were doing a roaring trade in Brighton!

My second job was in Bredon's Bookshop in East Street, which had an attractive small gallery on the first floor with a large bay window. Here we held exhibitions of pictures, with a new show every other month. They were very varied and included a fine show of Old Brighton prints, an unusual collection of model racing cars and oil paintings of cars. I went to the Redfern Galleries in Bond Street, London, and by prior arrangement chose 60 paintings by different artists, almost all of which were sold by the end of the exhibition.

Following a tremendous amount of organisation and hard work by my father, the builders and all the staff, both old and new, the Grand Hotel re-opened with a flourish on 10 October 1946. A long week-end of celebrations was planned and many of the regular pre-war guests and local dignitaries were invited.

Many of the pre-war visitors, who were notified well in advance (and of course all had to pay) came, beside local guests, many of whom had been regular 'day' visitors for the Christmas and Easter

150

special events. The architects and builders came, as well as the Mayor and Mayoress of Brighton and Hove, aldermen, councillors and several local hotel owners and managers. Also some of the heads of businesses who had supplied uniforms for the staff and most important, local food suppliers — people who had worked hard to obtain large quantities of the ingredients needed to produce a fabulous spread for the banquet — not so easy, as some food was still rationed. Last but not least, the wine merchants who supplied the vast amount of wine and spirits which the guests were expected to consume — and they did!

On the Thursday evening the banquet was held in the ballroom — decorated with Union Jacks, balloons and bunting — and everybody wore full evening dress. Pa was resplendent in his full regalia of tails and white tie, and Ma and I were in new, long evening gowns. All the ladies were given lovely corsages of carnations. There were plenty of speeches of congratulations, praise and thanks to all who had been involved in the huge achievement of restoring the Grand Hotel to its former pre-war glory. Then there was a spectacular ball with several hundred people dancing on the repaired and restored sprung dance floor, for which Ma and I wore yet more new evening dresses. At midnight there was a cabaret performed by dancers from a London West End show, popular at the time. More dancing continued until 2 a.m., when breakfast was served in the restaurant. A night to remember.

A couple of weeks before the great event, Pa asked me who I would like to invite as my escort. He must have been a little upset as I had not given the matter any thought. My closest male friend Desmond, the dentist, had very recently departed for Kenya for a long holiday to spend time with his parents who were living there — his father was a senior government advisor. Thus I hesitated as no one local came to mind. The following day Pa told me he had seen 'old Frank Wilson' and had arranged for 'young Frank Wilson' to escort me. I was not particularly pleased as I had never met this young man, but as there was to be a meeting of all the builders in my father's office the following day I went into Pa's office on some pretext, but really to look young Frank Wilson over! The room was very full of men and smoke and to my young eyes they all looked to be far too old to be Frank, though I learned afterwards he *was* there! In the end we had a very enjoyable two evenings together, at the banquet on the Thursday, when we found we had plenty to talk about and at the ball on the Saturday evening, when we much enjoyed dancing together.

Strange as it seems now, I then only saw him briefly on the few occasions when he came to functions in the hotel and was never aware of giving him much thought. A year or so later, however, we met again, danced together at the local tennis club and were engaged to be married shortly after.

Frank Wilson turned out to be quite the most exciting person I had ever met. We went to an army and navy ball in the Grand together soon after our engagement and when the dance ended neither of us were ready to go to our respective homes, so Frank suggested we went paddling in the sea. He was in full dress uniform, high boots and medals, and I was in my full-skirted, full-length evening gown. It was a beautiful night, very clear and a full moon shining on a calm sea and we ran down the beach across the pebbles to the sandy edge of the sea; even the tides were in our favour. We stood in the water and splashed each other. Quickly we got back into the car and drove to Hove Park, then, sitting in the back seat, snuggled together to get warm. A little while later there was a gentle tap on a window and there stood a smiling policeman who very politely said, 'It's gone 3 o'clock [in the morning], sir,' and (to me), 'I think your mother will be getting worried about you and you should remember what she has told you!' He was probably quite impressed by Frank's uniform because his remark was directed at me! He then smiled, said good-night and walked away. As we drove back to Cumnor Court I said, 'What on earth am I going to say to Ma?' Frank replied' 'Tell her the truth,' which I did and it worked — she must have been so amazed she said nothing!

Round about the same time we went together to a friend's wedding and towards the end of the proceedings Frank had an idea and

Frank Wilson

said, 'Let's go to Shoreham Airport and take Nicholas [his godson] up for a quick joyride.' Off we went and boarded the smallest plane imaginable and, with Nicholas on my knee and Frank chatting to the

153

pilot, we flew all over Brighton and Hove. I think by then I was almost speechless. It was my very first experience of flying and I could only nod in acknowledgement as Frank pointed out all the landmarks — the two piers, the Grand Hotel, his own home in Windlesham Gardens and endless other places, including where F.T. Wilson and Sons was working on various building contracts. Afterwards he kept saying to me, 'You did enjoy that didn't you, we must do it again?' I didn't say much during the flight, I was too terrified, so he mistook my stoic silence for bravery!

My marriage became a link between two Brighton builders, F.T. Wilson and Sons Limited and Jabez Reynolds, who was my great-grandfather. Wilson's was established in 1836 by William Wilson (which makes my son Robin a fifth generation of the Wilson family and his son Alasdair is, of course, the sixth). Above the main entrance to the old Brighton General Hospital, it reads 'Built by Jabez Reynolds — 1850'; the family business continued to flourish until 1886, when during a severe recession, Reynolds was owed so much money by his customers that he was forced into bankruptcy. His rival builder of the middle nineteenth century, F.T. Wilson's, continued and expanded until the severe economic depression of the late 1980s forced them into closure as well. A postscript to all this is that the offices belonging to Robin's accountancy firm (Wilson, Sandford and Co), located in Church Road, Hove, according to the deeds were built by Jabez Reynolds, his great-great grandfather.

There was more change in my life at that time, as soon after the Grand was reopened in 1946, Pa was appointed to the Board of Directors of Spiers and Ponds and about the same time he became General Manager and Director of the Spiers and Ponds Group. My parents were then able to live out of the Grand and they bought a flat in Dyke Road, and we were living there at Cumnor Court when I was married in September 1949.

I only recall a few details of our wedding. I would have preferred it to have been in a small country church — in fact, I had even chosen one — Westmeston Church near Ditchling, which had beautiful, blue stained-glass windows. But it wasn't to be. Instead, the

We are greeted by a 'lucky' sweep as we leave the Brighton College Chapel after our wedding in 1949

ceremony was in the chapel at Brighton College where Frank had been at school. On the day, both Pa and Frank had so many friends and business associates whom they felt compelled to invite, that there were many people there who I didn't even recognise! Also, we didn't know until some years later that we were very blessed, because a young man called Timothy Bavin sang with the choir. He later returned as vicar to my own church — the Church of the Good Shepherd in Brighton — and was a good friend. Subsequently he became Bishop of Johannesburg and later Bishop of Portsmouth. As tradition demanded, as we came out, a chimney sweep greeted us outside to wish us good luck, but Frank couldn't shake hands properly because he had broken his finger playing cricket the week before!

The reception was of course at the Grand, in the ballroom, with lots of speeches. A happy occasion, but Pa became quite agitated when told by the head waiter that the icing on the wedding cake was

Cutting the wedding cake at our reception in the Grand

Crowds of onlookers wish us on our way after our wedding

beginning to melt under the heat from the spotlights, so we had to hurry up and cut it — with Frank's regimental sword! We left early evening to drive to Newhaven for the night boat to France. The large crowd which gathered to see us off at the front entrance of the hotel was reminiscent of a film star's wedding — but of course this was cheap entertainment, as there was no television in those days!

On the very first day of my married life, lying in the top bunk, I opened my eyes to see the green slimy walls of Dieppe Harbour — with Frank still snoring in the bunk below — not very romantic! In 1949 France looked even shabbier than England, but the food was amazing compared with the food at home, where most things were still rationed. The warm Mediterranean Sea was especially wonderful to swim in after the cold English Channel. At that time restrictions on taking money out of England were still in force and we were only allowed £40 between us to cover our whole 4 weeks abroad. Pa still had connections in all the right places, though, and it was arranged we would collect extra French francs on our way through Paris at an address Pa had given to Frank. I well remember Frank parking his car outside a large building in the Place de la Concorde, leaving me there while he disappeared inside. I half imagined I would never see him again, such was the atmosphere of fear and uncertainty that remained in many large French cities for several years after the end of the war.

When we went to the casino in Monte Carlo, Frank managed to lose some of our precious francs at the gaming tables; that was the first time I was slightly cross with him. A large American warship was anchored in the harbour of Villefranche, not far from where we were staying in a hotel at Juan les Pins, and we met several groups of American sailors — why they were there in 1949 we never knew.

Returning home to Brighton, we rented a new modern house at the top of Ditchling Road, whilst F.T. Wilson and Sons were building our own house in Dyke Road Avenue, and we moved in there in 1950.

Myself and Peter with golden lab puppy Amber at our parents' flat

We led a fairly busy social life during the early years of our marriage. An annual event held in the Grand was the Naval and Military Ball and we always joined a group that included my old school friend

158

and her husband, Margaret and Basil Pett. Both Frank and Basil held senior rank and therefore we usually sat at the top table. Margaret and I were sitting either side of the General when, whilst she was having an animated conversation with him, one of her large dangling earrings came off and fell into the General's soup! Fortunately for us, particularly so because we got the giggles, he had a sense of humour and after a waiter had discreetly mopped away the soup and given him a fresh plate, order was restored and the formal dignified atmosphere returned.

Frank and I arriving at a Naval and Military Ball in the Grand Hotel ballroom

Dancing with Dick Braybon at a Naval and Military Ball (photograph from *The Sketch*)

Because of our age difference of eight years, Frank had seen much more of life than I, in spite of my five years in the WAAF. He had travelled extensively with his parents on the big cruise ships and all over Europe. As a boy he was an avid learner, always wanting to know more. The fact that he was an excellent linguist made our holidays to both France and Spain much more exciting. He was also a keen sportsman and played cricket and rugby for Brighton College and went on to play for three cricket clubs — St James', Brighton Brunswick and Preston Nomads. He enjoyed being in the Officer Training Corps (OTC) at the college and when he left, he joined the local TA RE (Territorial Army Royal Engineers) unit (119 Field Engineer Regiment). He was given his commission by King George V at a levy in Buckingham Palace — he told me this was the very last levy to be held. He was very much a 'man's man' and a leader, becoming a Justice of the Peace (JP) when he was only thirty-four and rising to the rank of full colonel.

Frank spent the early part of the war in France with the BEF (the British Expeditionary Force) and left about three weeks after Dunkirk after a difficult journey to Cherbourg, when he departed on the last boat to England. Initially he and his regiment were billeted in a hotel in Bournemouth for several weeks. He returned to France soon after D-Day in 1944, disembarking at Arromanche in Normandy on to the Mulberry harbour, which I believe he was involved in the construction of, before it was towed across the Channel. He was with the BAOR (British Army of the Rhine) in north west Europe until 1946, when he and his sappers spent much of the time building Bailey bridges over the rivers of northern France, to replace bridges which had been destroyed. This was often achieved when they were under heavy fire from the Germans.

Eventually, on reaching Belgium, the army ordered him to establish an Engineer Training School in the seaside resort of Knokke. His first contact with the local people was with the Mayor, Monsieur Verhulst, with whom he became very good friends. John Verhulst asked him back to his house for a drink to meet his wife and family. The son was in his mid-twenties and the youngest of the three daughters was a baby. When John telephoned his wife, 'Mama' Verhulst, she was so petrified at the idea of *any* soldier entering their home that she put Lulu into her pram and wheeled her into the wine cellar and shut the door. This sad little story tells us how terrifying the Germans' occupation of Europe was for ordinary decent people. Frank became close friends of the Verhulst family and we went together to visit them several times and to the family weddings. This friendship has stood the test of time and now my granddaughters are friends of John and Mama's great-grandchildren.

Frank was awarded an MBE and also held the decorations of Chevalier of the Order of Leopold II of Belgium and the Belgian Croix de Guerre.

161

20

An Eye-opening Trip to Post-war Germany

About four years after the war ended Pa needed to go to Germany to buy large quantities of wine for the hotel companies and he was keen that I should go with him. We drove to Bonn, where we stayed several nights and from there we visited Bad Neuenahr, where the then popular Apollinaires water was bottled. To my surprise I saw young boys, about nine or ten years old, sitting besides a long assembly line with hundreds of corks moving slowly past which they were sorting out, taking away any slightly damaged ones, the others moving on to be used as bottle tops. I was somewhat shocked to be told that child labour was still being used in central Europe.

During the time we were in Germany we were guests of the Deinhardt family, owners of the Deinhardt Wine Company, who also had offices in London. We were driven everywhere in one of their large black company cars by a chauffeur and escorted by a guide, who was able to speak a little English. Driving through Cologne was a memorable experience; the roads and pavements had been repaired and renewed, but everywhere beyond the inner boundary of the pavements were endless huge piles of rubble, although Cologne Cathedral was virtually untouched. It stood very high and proud, undamaged by bombs, as did our own St Paul's Cathedral in London during the Blitz.

One evening we attended a large banquet in Bonn Town Hall. Only two people spoke to us in English, and as we spoke no German it was a long and tedious occasion. Endless speeches, on and on, with no laughter, so presumably no jokes — very German!

We were taken by launch for several interesting trips down the Rhine and Mosel rivers, stopping at the riverside vineyards for wine-tasting sessions. These took place in cellars under the vineyards and the wines were delicious; it seems a pity to spit it out as one is obliged to during serious wine-tasting sessions!

During the second week of our visit we were invited to a private dinner party, held in the home of the senior Deinhardts, where we met their two sons and one of their two daughters. Both Herr and Frau Deinhardt spoke excellent English, having spent several years at the company's offices in London. Occasionally the conversation touched on the recent war and Frau Deinhardt told us that her elder daughter lived in Austria with her Austrian husband and three children. During the later part of the war she had been seriously worried about them — particularly the children, because Austria was in a bad way, and the family were almost starving. She made several journeys over the mountains, with a guide, taking as much food as she could carry and her husband explained that not only was it a very hazardous trip but also doubly dangerous because the Nazis had made a law forbidding civilian Germans to cross the frontier. The eldest son became somewhat agitated during this conversation and although he did not speak much English, it became obvious by his manner that he was a Nazi.

They also told us that Herr Deinhardt's brother had become a naturalised British citizen and that he was still the head of the family company's British branch of the business. His two sons had both been fighter pilots in the RAF, the eldest son having been killed. Quite extraordinarily the two cousins of the two sons, who were sitting with us at the table, had served in the Luftwaffe and may have unknowingly fought in air battles against their 'British' cousins.

Although the atmosphere had become somewhat tense during dinner it was an enjoyable and very interesting evening because the older generation could not have been more charming. Unfortunately, there was another side to all this, because the elder of the two sons, who were both unmarried, seemed to have taken a fancy to me. He was a very typical German, tall and blond with intense blue eyes, and an arrogant and conceited manner and he made me feel threatened. Thus when we arrived back at our hotel I asked my father to be sure he never left me alone with him. We were almost at the end of our visit, though, and fortunately Pa took my request seriously and all was well.

More than fifty years on, I believe my reflections on the conditions in Germany seen by Pa and myself in 1952 are worth mentioning.

During the earlier years of the Second World War the purpose of Bomber Command's campaign was to destroy anything of any military significance, such as armament factories, roads, railways, oil installations and industry in general. This was only partially successful for a variety of reasons. The High Command changed direction during the latter part of the war when the bombers began to focus more on total obliteration of the main towns and cities. The hope was that the bombing being carried out by the Americans and the British on the western front, in coordination with the huge losses being inflicted by the Russians on the eastern front, would destroy the morale of German civilians. Bomber Command's remarkable achievements and bravery of the aircrews and their huge losses of men and planes must never be forgotten. Without this sacrifice, the war would have lasted much longer.

Whilst we remember the dreadful human suffering and damage inflicted on our own cities, this was considerably less than that done by the allies to Germany. In May 1942 Cologne was attacked by a thousand-bomber raid and along with all other towns in the Ruhr Valley, continued to be a target. In spite of the inter-change of tourists and a number of sincere friendships between the British and the Germans, it will take several generations for those citizens to forgive and forget the Second World War.

Our visit in 1952, coming as it did so soon after the war had ended, made the warm welcome and the charm and generosity of the older Deinhardt family even more remarkable, but the hostility towards my own generation was very understandable.

For me as for many of my contemporaries, life seems to have been divided into two very different halves by the war — which changed so much. Before the war there was much class division and unemployment which caused great suffering for the working classes, and standards of behaviour were variable (as now). This was offset, however, by the respect felt by the great majority towards the professional classes — doctors, nurses, the legal profession, the church, politicians (in general) and teachers. On the whole the population felt more secure and safe within the perhaps limited boundaries of their lives.

The Second World War created, by necessity, rapid advances in technology. This made so many new things available — most of which were unknown before the war — such as television, washing machines, refrigerators, cars and flying all over the world. Perhaps most significant has been the development of the contraceptive pill, which has given women enormous freedom and career opportunities. Living as I did in the world of luxury hotels, however, I saw the wealth and comfort enjoyed by the guests, whilst at the same time I was very aware of the hard work and long hours worked by the hotel staff, a divide which existed before the war and in many ways continued after it was over.

21

New Beginnings

When we arrived home from Germany, both Frank and Ma were waiting for us in the sitting room of Cumnor Court, my parents' home in Dyke Road. During our holiday I had not felt particularly well and I was pretty sure I was pregnant. Ma remarked that I looked tired and should have an early night. Pa promptly announced I was going to present them with a grandchild in the spring — he was so excited that he sounded more like the prospective father. Of course both Frank and Ma were delighted but I was a little upset that I had not had the chance to tell my husband myself!

Frank and I were thrilled by the arrival of our son, Robin, and we proudly showed him off to the family when we gathered together at Cumnor Court to see the coronation of Queen Elizabeth II on the new black and white television Pa had bought for the event. Robin was three months old and his cousin Susan was due to arrive any moment. Peter and his wife Jean rushed off home rather suddenly after tea as her pains had started. I do recall a slight hiatus because Ma insisted they took so much food home with them. We had had a late lunch consisting of an elaborate cold collation (salads and cold meats) which was brought to the flat by a waiter from the Grand in a taxi!

The following year, when Robin was about eighteen months old, Pa kindly arranged for him and me to have a free holiday at Marsham Court in Bournemouth — another Spiers and Ponds hotel. He was an

Grandpa Reynolds with baby Robin and me

easy child and good company, but we both somewhat blotted our copy books on the day Pa drove down to take us back home. By then Robin was quite at home having his meals in the restaurant, sitting in a child's high chair, and enjoying being made a fuss of by the waiters. Pa had a longish discussion with him about what he would like to eat and eventually Robin chose grilled salmon (the most expensive item on the menu) and a baked potato. Pa was terribly proud of his grandson and Robin enjoyed all the attention from his grandfather. The waiters duly served his meal and asked if he would like the potato cut in half? Robin's response was to pick up the potato (perhaps to have a closer look), saying in a loud voice, 'This potato is BLOODY HOT!' I must have then endeavoured to regain control by cutting up the offending item, but my father was apoplectic with fury, saying, 'How dare you teach my grandson the appalling language you learned in the WAAF?' The moment soon passed, but I have never forgotten my poor father's horror, and what could the guests and staff have thought in that very public dining room?

In the early 1950s Pa asked F.T. Wilson's to build them a large bungalow near our own house in Dyke Road Avenue. Soon after they had moved in, Pa was very troubled by a take-over bid for the Spiers and Ponds Group. He did not like the people who would be responsible for the management, in particularly their attitude towards hotel staff. Very sadly this company, United Dairies, succeeded in buying all the hotels and he decided to retire. The whole scenario worried and upset him very much and his enforced retirement in his early sixties was a blow. He had been with the same company for about forty years, apart from two years or so of the war. His health began to deteriorate and he died far too young aged sixty-five. He was the longest serving Manager of the Grand Hotel and this record remains unbroken.

Frank remained Chairman of F.T. Wilson and Sons from the end of the Second World War until his death in 1969. Due to the difficult financial situation at the time, I was made Chairman of the company before his funeral — a very daunting task as I hadn't worked since I left Bredon's Art Gallery, twenty years previously. I believe I coped, not only because I had to with two young teenagers to support, but also because I was so angry at Frank's untimely death and in a strange way it was this anger (and probably the ability to 'put on a front' learned from my time in the hotel), which gave me the confidence to take on such a huge challenge. I was also enormously encouraged by the tremendous support I received from the staff — ordinary working men whose jobs depended on the survival of the company and several of whom became very good friends. I was only too aware of the responsibilities I had taken on and felt I had to 'rise to the occasion' for everyone's sake.

I have many memories of those incredibly interesting years but one incident in particular stands out. We had built the new Church Army Headquarters in Edward Street in Brighton and Margaret Thatcher had been invited to the official opening. I stood in a line with all the Directors of both F.T. Wilson and the Church Army — between our managing director and the architect — with my loyal son and daughter watching in the small crowd. I was introduced to

The reluctant businesswoman. I head off to a board meeting as Chair of F T Wilson & Sons Ltd

Mrs Thatcher as Chairman of the building company and she suddenly became very interested, and asked me how I came to be in the building trade. It seemed as though she had singled me out as a fellow 'business woman' as she asked me to show her around the very large building. I remember being very impressed with how she conducted herself during the visit and was delighted when she later became Prime Minister, despite my rather socialist leanings!

I continued to enjoy my role with F.T. Wilson for twenty years, when my son Robin took over as non-executive Chairman.

Although many years have passed since Frank died in 1969, much too young at the age of 54, I have always believed he is up there somewhere saying, 'Well done chaps' to Robin, Linda and me. His early death was a dreadful time for the three of us, but now I can look back and think how lucky I was to have been married to him for almost twenty years; how I wish, though, that he could have known his five grandchildren.

In 1980 I married again, to the childhood friend I had had a first date with in 1940! Sadly this did not work out well, and we separated in 1988. Since then I have had time to indulge in my much-enjoyed hobby of painting, now abandoned to write these witterings, which I hope will interest my five grandchildren and the few of my old friends who are still around!

22

Grand Celebrations and Reunions

Being eighty turned out to be much more exciting than I expected! To begin with, I decided if I was going to have a party there was only one place I really wanted to have it, in the place that I once called home — the Grand Hotel.

My grandchildren and their cousins had always shown so much interest in my reminiscences of the childhood that Peter and I spent in the hotel, but none of them had ever been inside the Grand. Robin, Linda and I discussed the possibility and our first concern was that the cost should be reasonable; therefore we could only invite family, a couple of school friends and my bridesmaids! In all we were about 30, which fitted in well to the Consort Room.

Linda and I arrived at about 11.30 a.m. and to our delight my brother Peter and all his family were already there. My three great-nephews, Ben, Jamie and Ollie, were standing in the main hall together, but I did not recognise them, thinking that they were three successful young business executives — I thought we must have got the date wrong! Niece Susan, their mum, had worked hard to persuade them out of wearing their jeans and trainers into smart suits and polished black shoes. That was my first lovely surprise; the next was the lovely flower decorations for the tables created by my daughter-in-law Fiona, who also took all the excellent photographs. Next there was a beautifully arranged display of family photographs and memorabilia put together by Linda.

A reunion of school friends and bridesmaids at my 80th birthday luncheon at the Grand. Left to right: Brenda, me, Margie and Joan

Everybody had arrived before 12.30 p.m. and we were all soon drinking champagne, with the party in full swing. Luncheon was a superb buffet, hot and cold choices, and we all tucked in and returned for seconds (even for thirds by some of the younger ones!). This was followed by informal speeches from brother Peter and son Robin, who were both eloquent and amusing — childhood memories from Peter, and from Robin, with his dry wit, some wry comments about his mother and uncle.

My son, Robin, entertains us at my 80th birthday luncheon

All the male guests then changed places so we could mix and have a chance to talk to everyone else. Meanwhile family entertainment was organised. Four grandchildren played various instruments (appreciated especially by son-in-law Ian who demonstrated his usual wicked sense of humour by putting cheese in his ears) and finally Susy highlighted key historical happenings since my birth in 1923. Next came the video (silent) of my wedding in the hotel in 1949, an extraordinary piece of history, which also gave my grandchildren a chance to see their grandfather, Frank, who sadly died so long ago; he looked so handsome. Then came the entry of the birthday cake, aglow with lighted candles. This was designed in three parts, the largest with 'Pamela' written on it, then two small sections with 'Happy 50th Robin' and 'Happy 21st Susy'. We ate all of the largest piece, accompanied by champagne, and I think Robin's cake and Susy's cake were taken home to eat later.

After tea I had the pleasure of giving my grandchildren and great-nephews and great-niece a small enamelled pill box which had a picture of the Grand Hotel in colour on the lid as a memento — and which I hope they each keep until they are eighty!

At that point, well past the time we expected to leave, it was suggested we should ask if we could all go up to see the rooms on the seventh floor which had been home. As there were not too many hotel visitors about (it being mid-January), the young assistant manager agreed to take us up. Great excitement, as several groups went up in the two lifts. Going into what had been very ordinary and dull rooms was quite a surprise, especially for Peter and me.

Everything was different; of course the whole area had been destroyed by the IRA bomb in 1984 and had been rebuilt. Our old sitting room was still a sitting room but now part of a very luxurious suite with bedroom and bathroom. But I couldn't help remarking, when we were told the cost of one night's stay, that in spite of all the expensive décor, when the gales blew in from the sea, it must still be as windy and noisy as Peter and I remembered!

We were up there quite a while and as an added attraction we looked out of the windows at the lights and the rusting ruin of the old

The family take a nostalgic trip to the seventh floor of the Grand to see where Peter and I spent our childhood, as photographed from the bottom of the amazing six-storey stairwell

West Pier, set off by an amazing sunset. Even after leaving the seventh floor, many of the family lingered, looking down over the ever-imposing stairwell, but Peter and I went down in the lift. Some weeks later, I was told several of the younger ones (I presumed) tried the 'spitting trick', which was retold yet again in my son's entertaining speech during lunch. It was some considerable time after that I was told the culprits were my daughter Linda and niece Susan, who were unable to resist having a go, having heard the story related so many times over the years. They then had to stop the younger generation follow their example — dear, dear, what a family!

My daughter, Linda, at the celebration at the Grand

Eventually we all went home. My party had lasted from 11.30 a.m. to 6.30 p.m. and in spite of being eighty I would have liked to have had it all over again!

Talking about the party the next day, brother Peter and I both said how very extraordinary it was that he and I had been allowed to roam all over the hotel when we were both so young, and how little our parents knew of what we got up to!

Peter and me by the Grand's glorious Christmas tree

Afterwords

Now in my eighties, I can look back and see how living in the Grand has influenced my life and, to a lesser degree, brother Peter's. Writing and remembering so much has been an enjoyable experience and I am fortunate to have a good memory.

The unusual location of my arrival in the world seems to have created a continuous thread of connections throughout the tapestry of my life, much of which would not have happened had I been born in an ordinary little house. It's as if my good fairy pointed me into all kinds of directions — some good and some not so good.

My being at ease, at lease superficially, with various situations has no doubt has been the result of a kind of confidence absorbed as a young person living in such an almost closed and restricted environment of extremes — knowing so many people from all walks of life. Perhaps so many different homes also made me more adaptable. On the other side of the coin, I am told my outward appearance of confidence sadly gives some people the impression I am snobbish and superior.

Certainly many people assumed we were very wealthy, living in the Grand, but that was not so. On occasions I have tried to contradict this view and explain that Father's salary took account of his family's board and lodging. Also that in spite of a large wedding in the hotel, I had started married life with only 10 shillings (50 pence) of my own in my post office account — and that did not increase until Ma died just before Frank some nineteen years later! Even within the family there were certainly petty jealousies. For example, Ma's two sisters, Auntie Dor-Dor and Auntie Ellie, thought that she was very lucky to have no housework or cooking to do. Of course during the war, living within the catering industry, we were not so much affected by food rationing as they had been.

In spite of the many restrictions, there was much that I liked and appreciated. Strangely, it is the actual building that stands out most in my memories and affections, particularly the feeling of security and warmth going into the huge old place always gave me. If I close my eyes, I can still see and feel the beautiful staircase — the smooth strong wood of the oak banisters, going round and round the high stairwell, particularly running my fingers over the carved circular newel post at the base. Then there was often the strong smell of expensive cigars and the rich aroma of pine needles on the huge Christmas trees — lovely!

Much has changed in the hotel, which is now even larger. Old adjoining properties have been knocked down and the hotel has been extended east and west, new public rooms added and the shapes of the old rooms altered. The furnishings and décor are very different. I loved the old, thick Turkish carpets and comfy armchairs. Guests have changed too. Casual dress of jeans, T-shirts and trainers is much in evidence and children run around, sometimes making a noisy nuisance of themselves — no longer 'seen, but not heard'!

The staff, though a new generation, are as charming and helpful as ever, but oh dear, everyone calls everyone else by their Christian names, nobody seems to be called 'Sir' or 'Madam' anymore. Pa would have been horrified!

My father was a 'grand hotelier' of a very special type — friendly and kind towards all staff and guests, but able to keep control of such a large operation and the respect of all by his very 'hands-on' management. He instinctively knew every detail of the jobs done by the staff and the needs of the guests. Always being wherever he was needed and aware of the range of complexities created by such large numbers of people living and working closely together.

Fortunately, Ma — one of whose favourite maxims was, 'There is good in everybody' — was a fairly relaxed sort of lady, tender hearted towards guests and staff. It cannot have always been easy. She would have had little in common with the rather elderly lady residents, mostly very wealthy widows. Human nature being what it is, there would have been times when they found fault, perhaps with the staff or the with way things were done — the latter reflecting on my father. In fact Pa was also very patient with these particular guests, who often turned to him for advice and support. To my knowledge, Ma had only one close friend, a cousin on her father's side, 'Auntie Kitty', who lived in Brighton with her husband and two sons.

There have been a number of occasions when the ambivalent attitude of both family and friends has been a little hurtful. Understandably, they often implied how fortunate I was to live in such obvious luxury and with so much apparent wealth. Few would have understood what a restricted childhood we were forced to lead, always supposed to be on our best behaviour. There was almost nowhere we could let off steam and make a noise and we were very aware of how much we longed to have our own garden.

Peter's life has been very different. Although he made good friends in the hotel, he never really liked living there. He must have inherited Mother's love of animals and nature, and from a young age always wanted to be a farmer.

Despite the obvious limitations on us as children of living in the hotel, this strange and sometimes exotic childhood was a special experience which must have widened our horizons. If it hadn't been for the extraordinary location of my birth and upbringing I probably wouldn't have met and married either my first husband, Frank or my second husband, Kenneth. Nor would I have had our wedding reception there, nor my fabulous eightieth birthday party. I am fortunate indeed that my home was a Grand Hotel.

Dates

1820	King George IV (formerly Prince Regent) crowned and visits Brighton
1821	Brighton's Royal Pavilion completed
1830	William IV crowned
1836	**FT Wilson & Sons Ltd established in Brighton (building company)**
1837	Victoria crowned
1841	September — First train pulls into Brighton station (first-class passengers only)
1864	The Grand Hotel opens
1865	West Pier opens
1893	**5 December – Vera Madeleine Reynolds is born**
1896	**12 January — Sidney T Smith is born**
1901	Edward VII crowned
1910	George V crowned
1920	**September — Marriage of Sidney and Vera**
1923	**15 January — Pamela Sydney Smith is born in the Grand Hotel**
1926	The General Strike
1927	**30 November — Peter Arthur Sidney Smith is born in Hove**
1936	George VI crowned following abdication of the uncrowned Edward VIII
1939	3 September — War declared on Germany
1940	May — Dunkirk
1940	**July – The Grand Hotel closes. Family moves to Hans Crescent Hotel, London**

1940	8 August to 10 October – Battle of Britain
1940	2 September — London Blitz begins
1940	**November — Hans Crescent Hotel bombed**
1940	**December — Move to Valley of the Rocks Hotel, Lynton**
1941	**30 October — Reported for service in the WAAF, Innsworth, Devon**
1941	**November — Morecambe Bay, Lancashire**
1941	6 December — Pearl Harbour attacked, USA joins the allies
1941	**December — 11 Group, Fighter Command, Uxbridge**
1943	**February — Kenley (Surrey), Uxbridge & Capel-le-Ferne (Folkestone)**
1943	**Autumn — 100 Group, Bomber Command Bylaugh Hall, Norfolk**
1944	6 June — 'D' Day landings in Normandy
1945	**WAAF — 11 Group, Fighter Command, Uxbridge**
1945	7 May — VE Day
1945	12 September — VJ Day
1946	**8 February — Discharge from the WAAF (last day 14 December 1945)**
1946	**10 October — The Grand Hotel re-opens**
1949	**24 September – Marriage to Frank Wilson, Grand Hotel, Brighton**
1953	Coronation of Queen Elizabeth II
1961	**13 February – Sidney T Smith dies**
1968	**8 December – Vera Madeleine Smith dies**
1969	**14 May – Frank Wilson dies, Pamela becomes Chair of FT Wilson & Sons Ltd**
1980	**16 May – Marriage to Sir Kenneth Newton, Guildford**
1984	12 October — IRA bomb at the Grand Hotel
1986	28 August — The Grand Hotel re-opens
1988	The Grand Hotel becomes the first 5 star hotel in Brighton
2001	15 February — Brighton and Hove awarded city status
2003	**Pamela's 80th birthday luncheon, Grand Hotel, Brighton**
2008	***Home was a Grand Hotel* is published**